"One ... provo... ... and f... ing for ... extrao... undertaking.
—Richard Knowlton, chairman, president, and chief executive officer, Geo. A. Hormel & Co.

"A great book! ... Millions of us are caught up in workaholic cycle, to our great loss. Bob Larrañaga's work is a valuable tool in overcoming the false prophets within, demanding more, and learning to be gentle with ourselves."
—Earnie Larsen, author of *Stage II Recovery, Stage II Relationships*, and *Days of Healing, Days of Joy*

"*Calling It a Day* is so important in helping us to see how we can work smarter and healthier."
—Harvey Mackay, author of *Beware the Naked Man Who Offers You His Shirt*

"Larrañaga has identified the major bugaboos—control, time, ambition, and others—that confine and rule the workaholic.... The borrowed wisdom alone—in pithy quotes—is worth the investment in this book."
—Cathy Madison, senior editor, *Adweek*

"An outstanding book.... Easy to read ... worth studying carefully, reflecting upon, and savoring."
—Peter H. Engel, president, Porosan Leasing, Inc., and author of *The Overachievers*

"Paragraph after paragraph, chapter after chapter of Mr. Larrañaga's book hits the hardworking business executive right between the eyes. At the end of each page, I said to myself—that's me."
—Sidney J. Feltenstein, Jr., senior vice president, Dunkin Donuts

CALLING IT A DAY

Daily Meditations for Workaholics

Robert Larrañaga

1817

Harper & Row, Publishers,
San Francisco

New York, Grand Rapids, Philadelphia, St. Louis
London, Singapore, Sydney, Tokyo, Toronto

All Bible quotations were taken from the *New American Bible*, Catholic Book Publishing Co., Washington, D.C., 1970.

Cartoon caption taken from a John Louthan "Briefcase" cartoon, copyright ©1989, Universal Press Syndicate.

Bishop Sheen anecdote reprinted with permission of *The Executive Speechwriter Newsletter*.

FIRST EDITION

Library of Congress Cataloging-in-Publication Data

Larrañaga, Robert
    Calling it a day : daily meditations for workaholics / Robert Larrañaga—1st ed.
       p.   cm.
    Includes bibliographic references.
    ISBN 0–06–250512–2
    1. Workaholics—Prayer-books and devotions—English.
    2. Devotional calendars.   I. Title.
    BV4596.W67L37 1990
    242'.68—dc20   89–45986
                                                              CIP

---

90 91 92 93 94 K.P. 10 9 8 7 6 5 4 3 2 1

This edition is printed on acid-free paper that meets the American National Standards Institute Z39.48 Standard.

To Mary,
who always has her priorities straight

CONTENTS

PREFACE

Work is part of the human condition. It is at the very core of our existence. The work of survival consumes about 3,800 BTUs of energy every hour of our lives. We can't escape work, nor should we want to. We *Homo sapiens* are problem-solving, tool-fashioning, working animals. Science, invention, art, music, and poetry are the most sublime expression of our very need to work.

Only when work becomes compulsive, unfeeling behavior, seemingly devoid of choice, does it become inhuman. When we work twelve to fourteen hours a day, six days a week, week in and week out, we become workaholics.

Workaholics are high-energy people with a strong need to dominate and control. Impulsive and time sensitive, we can be demanding, aggressive, and quick-tempered. At the same time, our quicksilver attention span and aversion to risk can lead to vacillation and unfocused activity. We always do more than the situation requires. Our motto seems to be "If it's worth doing, it's worth overdoing."

At the same time, we're often considered inspiring, motivating executives who add to our company's momentum. Our department is where the action is, at least for a while.

But no one can continue at the pace we set for ourselves. Eventually the fun goes out of work, and we become grimly determined to win at all costs, keeping score with dollars, counting perks and prestige symbols as extra points.

By this point, working for the sake of work consumes every available hour. It disrupts our home life, affects our health, and leaves us feeling burned out (As one workaholic put it, "*Tired* is my middle name.") Eventually, we become cynical, bitter, and despondent. We may rely on drugs, alcohol, and coffee to keep us going during the day, and be so keyed up we can't sleep at night. We are among the working wounded.

If all this sounds familiar, you may be one of us and wondering what to do about your workaholism.

Of all the forms of compulsive behavior (such as gambling or drinking), workaholism is unique. First of all, you *have* to work. You can't avoid it if you want a roof over your head, clothing on your back, and food on the table. Secondly, in our culture, a strong work ethic is seen as a virtue to be admired, in sharp contrast to other compulsions. Third, your compulsive, self-destructive behavior is rewarded by success—the big house with the three-car garage, the foreign sports car in the driveway, country club membership, and vacation condo. The only thing missing from the picture is you—you're at the office, working late.

Breaking your workaholic habit won't be easy. Unfortunately, there are no well-organized support groups for workaholics; and, if there were, the members would probably work too hard at making them a success. Don't expect a sympathetic ear from your boss, either. If he or she hears that you are cutting back on your hours, you may be labeled a "shirkaholic."

In today's corporate culture, the emphasis is on running lean and mean and working harder. The new management ethic calls for fewer employees, each handling a heavier, more stressful workload. In one survey of three thousand managers, 30 percent said they were feeling more stress this year than last.

The good news is, you're not imagining the problem; the bad news is, it's going to get worse. In the next ten years, the factors feeding into your workaholism will increase inexorably. Changes in society, business, and technology will add to the strain you're feeling now, and you'll be forced to accept that the harder you work, the more behind you get.

As a result of the babyboom generation, there is an oversupply of middle-level managers, which has significantly increased competition in the job market. You find yourself working harder to keep your place in the corporate hierarchy. In fact, 25 to 30 percent of middle-management jobs will turn over this year and many of the displaced executives will discover, to their chagrin, that employers are looking for executives between the ages of twenty-five and thirty—with forty years' experience.

At the same time, a real labor shortage looms among the next generation, so middle managers are caught in a tightening vise. You have more to do and no one to delegate it to.

Another factor contributing to the rise in workaholism is rapid technological advances in fast-growing fields such as aerospace and computers. In those industries, knowledge has a half-life of about three years, and people who don't run to stay in place, are thrown from the treadmill. Entrepreneurs who seize on the new technology are often among the most compulsive workaholics in that they seem to have a messianic zeal to bring their labor-saving devices to the world.

Finally, the restructuring of U.S. industry through mergers, acquisitions, and leveraged buyouts, combined with sharp swings in the money markets, interest rates, and inflation, has placed tremendous pressures on executives at every level. Under the circumstances, it's surprising that there aren't more workaholics.

Business executives are not the only ones suffering from workaholism. Their families are often victimized by a behavior pattern that is difficult to fathom. The workaholic takes the family on an emotional roller coaster ride, through the peaks and valleys of a high-speed career, always on track, but somehow out of control. It makes no difference who is in the front seat of a roller coaster: everyone gets butterflies and vertigo.

If you are truly fortunate, you may be able to get the support you need from your family in dealing with your workaholism. But in the final analysis, it is your problem, and you will have to deal with it on your own terms. That's where this book may help.

Calling It a Day is a Twelve-Step self-help book for workaholics. It follows many of the same principles that have proven helpful in coping with other forms of compulsive behavior, such as alcoholism. It describes attitudes and personality traits that may contribute to your workaholism and provides business practices and spiritual principles you can adapt to your situation.

The book is organized into twelve chapters, paralleling the twelve months of the year, each chapter dealing with a specific aspect of workaholism. Within each chapter, one theme is developed in a series of daily meditations. The readings can be meditated on in chronological sequence, or according to the subject uppermost in your mind each day.

To get the most out of the book, find a quiet, comfortable spot where you can meditate without interruption for fifteen to twenty minutes a day. Pick a time when you are alert, yet relaxed. As thoughts occur to you, enter them in a journal so that you can reflect on them later with the perspective afforded by the passage of time. Gradually you'll develop a new insight into yourself and your attitudes about work and leisure. As your thought patterns change, so too should your work patterns change. The very fact that you are spending fifteen to twenty minutes a day in meditation automatically increases your leisure time!

But workaholism is a lifelong struggle, and there is no such thing as a cure. In order to progress, you will have to make a permanent commitment to a program such as the one outlined in this book. The good news is "By the Lord are the steps of a man made firm and he approves his way" (Psalm 37:23). So long as you are taking steps to cope with the problem, you are going in the right direction.

JANUARY

Control

In the business world, the one unpardonable sin is the admission that our jobs have become unmanageable. We are conditioned to believe that we must have total control over every aspect of our work. If workaholics accept this message as gospel, it's because we have a strong need to control our own destiny. On the one hand, we rebel against authority; on the other hand, we insist on total control over our subordinates. As a result, we are frequently in conflict with superiors and peers. Our first step is to admit that our need for total control has made our lives unmanageable.

JANUARY 1

*"If you're not here on Saturday, don't
bother showing up for work on Sunday."*
—Sign in an ad agency art department

In ancient Greece and Rome, slaves had a
hundred holidays a year, more days off than many
executives take in the headlong pursuit of success.
If you're a senior executive, you probably work over
fifty seven hours a week. Your problem isn't simply
one of long hours, however, it's also one of frenetic,
mind-numbing activity. Chances are you attend five
meetings a day and return to a cluttered desk and
bulging "in" basket, only to be interrupted once
every twelve minutes.

Reflections:

Which of us hasn't wished at some time that we
could turn our back on success, quit our job with
dignity, don bib overalls, and carve wooden birds
for a living? If only life were that simple. The truth
is that, as workaholics, we'd probably be mass-pro-
ducing wooden birds in no time! You see, the problem is not with our job; it's our attitude. Somehow,
we have convinced ourselves that it's not enough to
be in charge—we have to be in control. But, the
more we try to control, the greater our frustration
and disappointment become.

The only thing I can control is my outlook on life.

JANUARY 2

"Not everything that is more difficult is more meritorious."
— Thomas Aquinas

Some executives think that a balanced approach to work means having two briefcases, one in each hand. They never have enough time to get their work done. There is always one more memo to write, one more budget to recap, one more deadline to meet. Just when they see the top of their desk, the afternoon mail arrives, and the cycle begins anew. At the end of the day, they sweep the contents of their desk into the gaping maw of a briefcase and head for home, resolved to get control of their work load. It never happens.

Reflections:

Workaholism, like any habit, is situational in that there are factors in our work place that reinforce our behavior, sometimes subtly and subconsciously, but decisively. For example, is a large briefcase sitting next to your desk waiting to carry home any unfinished work? Chances are it contains memos and reports that you've meant to read and have carried back and forth for days. Each time you put something in that briefcase, you're admitting you're out of control.

Today I will buy a small portfolio to replace my briefcase.

JANUARY 3

"A clean desk is the sign of a cluttered mind."

—Anonymous

A neat, well-organized desk is usually a sign that someone is on top of his or her work load. But it can also be a sign of stagnation. Your zeal for control can result in such scrupulous attention to neatness that you bog down in trivia. Your truly important projects are put off while you straighten up your desk, answer routine correspondence, rearrange files, and sharpen your pencils. Your desk is neat, but your priorities are messed up, and you have lost control of your time.

Reflections:

Like it or not, a certain amount of chaos goes with the job. You can organize every drawer and label all your files, but in one week they'll be messy again. A cluttered desk and messy cabinet are the handiwork of entropy, the second law of thermodynamics. The law of entropy says that all closed systems drift toward chaos—and that includes your office. Willard Gibbs, founder of Chemical Thermodynamics, put it this way over a hundred years ago: "Within the universe, order is the least probable state." Why not cluster all your trivia in one brief span each day? You can read, toss, or file it faster if you handle it all at once.

I'm going to ignore my low-priority mail until late in the day.

JANUARY 4

"What counts is not the number of hours you put in, but how much you put in the hours."

—Anonymous

When it comes to filekeeping, workaholics are without peer. We put *everything* in writing. To us, they're not just memos, letters, and reports; they're "insurance," our protection against life's uncertainties, evidence of our control—we have it in writing, "just in case." Our obsession with covering ourselves in writing has contributed to a threefold increase in the consumption of writing and printing paper in the past thirty years. Each four-drawer file we create costs $25,000 and another $2,160 annually to maintain. Yet 75 to 85 percent of the documents over one year old are never referred to again. No matter—we *feel* like we're in control.

Reflections:

Obviously you need a good filing system, but the key to filing is knowing what to save, how to save it, and for how long. Management experts recommend cleaning files twice a year, throwing out unessential, outdated items. Holding on to outdated files is a sign of excessive control. In the end, the system itself becomes time consuming and unmanageable. Cluttered files simply add to your stress.

Tossing out my old files can be great "therapy."

"Today, if you're not confused, you're not thinking clearly."

—Irene Peters

Workaholics are compulsive information seekers. We equate information with power and control. But our underlying assumption is wrong because information does not lead to control. If the era of DNA and RNA has one lesson for us, it is that information is the organizing principle that leads to ever-increasing complexity. There is always one more messy fact, one more doubt to be satisfied, before we feel in control.

Reflections:

Information overload is a leading stressor among workaholics. Our brains can only control so much information at one time. According to Martha H. Rader of Arizona State University, we can deal with seven bits of information simultaneously, and, anything greater has to be chunked together in groups of three or four for ease of manipulation and recall. Computers, of course, don't have these limitations. They churn out strings of facts and figures in ever-increasing degrees of complexity. The next time you feel overwhelmed by all the data, why not get out from behind your computer to talk to the front-line people?

Accepting my limitations is the beginning of wisdom.

JANUARY 6

"Nothing is stronger than habit."

—Ovid

Many successful people cling to "habitudes" developed when they were young, struggling entrepreneurs, surviving by their wits. A habitude is a behavior that is no longer appropriate. Your habitude might be to open all incoming mail, sign every purchase order, save every paper scrap, and sharpen every pencil right down to the nub. Whatever it is, at one time it had survival value, but now it is an anachronism and an outward sign of every workaholic's fear: something terrible is going to happen. Your good fortune can't last, catastrophe awaits! Only the spartan shall survive.

Reflections:

A need to control every detail of your business affairs may have seemed essential earlier in your career; but when your responsibilities widen, certain details can become distractions. If you still focus on them, examine your underlying motives. It could very well be that you're afraid to enjoy your success because it might tempt the fates. In your heart of hearts, you may not feel deserving of all you've achieved. To compensate for feelings of unworthiness, you may overdo everything.

I'm going to break my habitudes by thinking bigger.

JANUARY 7

"To err is human, to forgive is not company policy."

—Anonymous

As the central metaphor of our time, the computer shapes the way we conduct business. We are mesmerized by its speed and accuracy, appreciate its responsiveness and dependability, and unconsciously mimic its performance. We follow routines and subroutines, think in terms of decision trees and PERT charts and "interface" with employees who "download" the data we need to "address" a problem. In internalizing the rational, logical computer model, we deny our emotions, and function like automatons, says Craig Brod, author of *Technostress*.

Reflections:

Workaholics are easily seduced by the speed of the computer. We equate thinking faster with thinking smarter and assume that the power of the computer increases our control. But in multiplying our ability to process information, the computer also expands our concept of what we can and should control. The pressure to perform increases at the same time that we become more rigid and machinelike. We insist on instant, error-free answers and fly into a rage if others act human. We lose our sense of humor. If you can't crack a joke, you may be ready to crack.

Today I'll take time to banter and joke with other employees.

JANUARY 8

In the information era, we consume facts, figures, and ideas at such an incredible rate that anyone who isn't computer literate is committing "datacide." But being informed is not the same as knowing. Information becomes knowledge only when we are able to organize it according to our own mental framework and reason by analogy to a new level of understanding. In this sense, all knowledge is subjective: we give new meaning to the facts.

Reflections:

We simply cannot absorb and process all the information being produced as raw data by the millions of computers in today's work place. Overwhelmed by the task, we career out of control from one fact-filled meeting to the next. In an effort to cope, we narrow our focus and develop tunnel vision; but, in so doing, we lose sight of the wider context, the "soft data," and our thinking becomes rote and unimaginative. Take the time today to turn off your computer and exchange ideas with your coworkers.

May I never forget that the things that count the most can't be counted.

JANUARY 9

"So much has been written about everything that you can't find out anything about it."

—James Thurber

In a remarkably short period, fax machines became prominent features of the business scene. U.S. fax sales rose from 191,000 units in 1986 to over a million today. Following close behind the fax machine is electronic mail. A decade ago, there were 10,000 electronic mailboxes; today there are six million and the number of electronic messages could soon top a billion. The emergence of the "telecommunity" extends our ability to control events without face-to-face dialogue. But you can't manage by remote control. You have to get out from behind your computer.

Reflections:

The office is more than a place in which to work. It's where you spend nearly one-third of your adult life. You make friends, engage in good-natured bantering and pranks, share hopes and dreams, console and comfort others. In many respects, your co-workers are your extended family. You need a certain amount of face-to-face interaction with them. If you're too absorbed in work and too busy for a coffee break, you're out of control. Turn your computer off long enough to ask someone, "What's new?"

Today I'm going to "manage by walking around."

> *"In times like these, it helps to recall that there have always been times like these."*
>
> —Paul Harvey

U.S. Steel, U.S. Rubber, United Aircraft, Cities' Service, R. J. Reynolds, Standard Oil, Westinghouse Broadcasting, Del Monte—all these once familiar corporate names have disappeared from the Fortune 500. Historically, ten of the Fortune 500 change their name each year as a result of mergers, acquisitions, expansion, or contraction. The corporate staffs do not exert as much control over their destiny as their glossy annual reports might suggest. In fact, the only thing any of us can really control is our response to change.

Reflections:

One of the significant changes occurring in U.S. business is the number of executives returning to school, taking home study courses, and attending self-improvement seminars. Each year over a million people are purchasing self-help audio cassettes on everything from stress management to negotiating skills. If you haven't already tapped this valuable resource, make a commitment to yourself today to look into it. Mind-stretching exercises can keep you limber enough to adapt to change.

Today I'm going to buy a self-improvement cassette for my car.

*"If you have a job without aggravations,
you don't have a job."*
—Malcolm Forbes

Falling sales, rising overhead, trickling cash flow—any one of the problems can dominate your thinking and take control of your life, if you let it. Why not reread your files from the same period last year, when (chances are) you faced similar problems. Business is cyclical, and time has a way of changing your perspective. With the help of hindsight, you can see that you've been through this before. The specific circumstances may differ, but the broad outlines are the same. Things can work out again.

Reflections:

In our need for control, we abhor uncertainty. We need to know the outcome in advance. When the answers to our problems aren't swift in coming, we lose patience with prayer and act impulsively, often making our predicament worse. If you find yourself becoming impatient with your Higher Power's timing, release the anxiety that lies coiled like a spring inside you, waiting to snap. Reread your files to see how you've handled similar problems, and to bolster your self-confidence. Pray for peace of mind.

My Higher Power and I together can do anything that I can't do alone.

"The secret of good management is: no surprises."

—Harold Geneen

To workaholics, a surprise, even a pleasant one, is unsettling because it signals that something is not under control. Unfortunately, life is full of surprises. Pay phones don't work when you need to make an urgent call. Airplanes never leave on schedule—unless you're stuck in a traffic jam near the terminal. And copier machines break down the morning your proposal is due. Despite these nagging reminders of our fallibility, we cling to the illusion that total control is only a computer keystroke away.

Reflections:

Computer technology has greatly extended our span of control. But it has also increased our span of error! Trying to run a business with spreadsheets is like reading sheet music for a symphony and trying to imagine how it would really sound. To fully appreciate the music, you have to hear it played. To orchestrate the activities of a company, you have to get beyond bar charts and graphs and listen to your suppliers, customers, and employees. If you're not in tune with them, you're in for a surprise.

I can avoid surprises by staying close to the market.

*"Certitude is not the test of certainty. We
have been cocksure of many things that
just weren't so."*
—Oliver Wendell Holmes

A strong need to feel in control of events can
lead you to reduce everything to its simplest and
therefore most manageable terms. One clear sign of
oversimplification is "tabloid thinking," in which
you make bold, sweeping statements that aren't sup-
ported by a closer reading of all the facts. This sort
of stark, black-and-white reasoning usually confuses
causation with correlation or coincidence.

Reflections:

As controlling personalities, we favor rules, for-
mulas, and laws whose operations are predictable.
At the same time, we tend to ignore the exceptions
to the rule because they complicate matters. But the
fact remains that many things correlate without having a causal connection, and coincidence does play
a role in our business affairs. For example, statistics
show that the average executive works 42.5 hours a
week. But it does not follow that you will be 10
percent more successful just because you work 47
hours a week.

I'm going to avoid jumping to conclusions.

JANUARY 14

> *"The demand for certainty is one that is natural to man, but is nevertheless an intellectual vice."*
> —Bertrand Russell

Workaholics often live in a world of absolutes where there are no halfway measures. Everything is black and white, no messy shades of gray. But the subtlty of reality frustrates our search for absolute certainty, even in something as simple as the choice of color for the cover of a report. For example, black and white are part of all other colors, including each other. Black and white are opposite, yet the same.

Reflections:

The truth comes in many shades of red, blue, green, and gray, but our schooling conditions us to think in terms of absolutes such as "true" and "false," "black" and "white." The challenge we face as workaholics is to open our minds to new ways of thinking and other points of view. There are at least two sides to every story, and in many cases it is not a question of which side is true; it's simply a matter of degree. Neils Bohr, the Nobel laureate, put it this way: "A great truth is a statement whose opposite is also true."

Today I'm going to keep my mind open and my mouth closed.

"You cannot be friends on any other terms than upon terms of equality."
—Woodrow Wilson

Maybe you're not depressed, but you could be repressed. We workaholics bottle up our emotions in order to appear in control at all times. But repressed feelings find expression in other ways, such as restless, frenetic activity; forgetting appointments; leaving briefcases on planes; missing deadlines; failing to return phone calls; and having accidents. Your troubled spirit vents its anger at you. You need someone with whom you can share your problems, but that is difficult for a manager to do.

Reflections:

A good manager doesn't share problems with subordinates unless they can contribute to the solution; otherwise, he or she merely upsets subordinates. At the same time, it is difficult to share feelings with a peer who is a friendly competitor for the next promotion. Nor can you share openly and honestly with the boss you're trying to impress. Yet you must find someone—possibly a friend, family member, or a minister—to whom you can confide your innermost feelings. Find someone who, above all, is a good listener.

I'm going to talk out my troubles with a friend.

JANUARY 16

"A friend to all is a friend to none."
—Aristotle

Most workaholics are outgoing people with many acquaintances; however, we have few close friends because friendships take time to develop, and we never have enough time. Friendship also requires intimate sharing, and we prefer to keep people at a distance. For example, consider all the names in your pocket address book—how many of the people in it know one another personally? In many cases, the only thing they have in common is you. Do you have a circle of friends? Or, do you have a broker. A banker. An insurance agent. Doctor. Auto mechanic.

Reflections:

A willingness to share is at the very core of all lasting friendships. In extending a handshake, you give someone else a claim on your life and release your own grip—your control—over your free will. As long as you feel the need to control others, you won't feel like you're part of the group. We all need to feel that we belong to a support group, especially during times of stress. Is there one person in your pocket address book you can call today to share how you're feeling now?

I'm going to call an acquaintance who has reached out to me as a friend.

> "Laughter is the shortest distance between two people."
>
> —Victor Borge

When you sit on a task force, you soon discover that each member has a separate agenda. At times, the committee minutes seem so different from the session you attended that you have to check the distribution list to make sure you were there. Sure enough, there's your name, but nowhere is there any mention of your penetrating insights, your statesman-like remarks. Upsetting? You bet. But not nearly as upsetting as it might be if you interrupt the dialogue and start dictating to the group.

Reflections:

A workaholic's management style is often one of rigid autocratic policymaking, which stifles initiative and discourages the open, freewheeling exchange of ideas. If your subordinates aren't questioning you and challenging some of your decisions, it could well be that the atmosphere in your company or department is as stifling as a room without a thermostat. Open the windows, and let the sunshine in. Remember, the role of a committee chairman is to make the members laugh once every fifteen minutes.

Instead of being "all business," I'm going to be all smiles.

JANUARY 18

*"Nothing is more dangerous than an
idea, when a man has only one idea."*
—Alain

Controlling personalities can be very stubborn;
they cling to a position long after it has been under-
mined by new information. Rather than change their
mind, they may question the source of facts or the
way in which the facts were compiled. If all else
fails, they may defend their position on "principle".
The truth is, they are reluctant to change their position and admit they were wrong.

Reflections:

All of us make mistakes. Effective managers are
willing to reexamine their decisions, in light of new
information, and quickly change their mind. Their
self-esteem isn't threatened by a simple error in
judgment. They merely learn from it and move on.
The fact is: if you make a bad decision, you get to
make another one.

*I'm going to be open to new ideas and new ways of
doing business.*

*"The process of scientific discovery is, in
effect, a continual flight from wonder."*
—Albert Einstein

At one point in the Apollo space program, mission control asked the astronauts who was in control of the space craft, and the answer that came back was "Newton." For three centuries, Newtonian physics has guided our exploration of the world. But now, as we stand ready to conquer the heavens, the earth opens beneath our feet to reveal a dark void, a quantum realm, where the laws of physics no longer work, and Newton is no longer in control.

Reflections:

On the quantum level, we've reached a point where science can observe but it cannot measure with certainty. It's a place where physics and metaphysics meet, and where all we can do is wonder at the mysteries of creation. Like the astronauts orbiting effortlessly in outer space, we have to let go and accept that, on the most elemental level, we are not in control—our Higher Power is.

I'm going to let go and let God.

JANUARY 20

> "The handwriting on the wall may be a
> forgery."
>
> —Ralph Hodgson

Total control is an illusion; not even history's
most powerful monarchs had absolute control. For
example, on the morning of July 14, 1789, King
Louis XVI of France wrote in his diary a single
word, rien, "nothing"—as if "nothing" would happen on the very day that history would record as
Bastille Day! Industrial rulers are no better at controlling their fate. The average tenure for the chief
executive of a Fortune 500 company is only six
years.

Reflections:
You can create a detailed analysis of your company's strengths and weaknesses, correctly evaluate
your competition, and set realistic goals. But no
matter how thorough your plan appears, there will
always be an unknown variable that lies outside
your control. Contingency planning, financial controls, and management procedures can reduce the
risk, but they can't eliminate it. History suggests
that the charts and graphs in the overhead transpar-
encies flashed on the wall in a strategy session are
an illusion. The best any of us can hope for is that
we do our best.

Come what may, I will do my best.

"He who does not open his eyes must open his purse."
—German proverb

For over two hundred years, the house of Rothschild financed Europe's wars and was privy to the most sensitive secrets of state. During the Napoleonic wars, while England anxiously awaited news of the campaign, Nathan Rothschild entered London's Stock Exchange and suddenly began selling all his stock. Instantly, rumor spread of a British defeat, panic gripped the exchange, and stock prices plummeted. Meanwhile, Rothschild's agents quietly bought back many stocks at the panic prices. When word arrived from France, the speculators discovered what Rothschild knew all along: the British had won. The value of Rothschild's stocks soared.

Reflections:

Rothschild never said Britain had lost; he didn't have to, because he knew how people would interpret his actions. In a deteriorating situation where things seem out of control, we tend to overreact. This is especially true of workaholics because of our need for control and stability. Too late, we learn the importance of remaining cool and calm in a crisis.

Things are rarely as serious as I make them seem.

"Never tell people how to do things. Tell them what to do, and they will surprise you with their ingenuity."
—George S. Patton

How often do your managers update you on their projects? The frequency with which you get progress reports may indicate how you control your work. If managers report back to you on every decision, things may be getting out of control. Your situation is analogous to that of a battlefield commander: when the army advances, the lines of communication stretch, and messengers take longer to reach the commander; but when the troops retreat, messengers from the front stumble over one another in their rush to report the bad news.

Reflections:

As workaholics, our need for control is such that we may welcome the close interaction with subordinates and require them to check with us before taking any actions. But the best instruction is often simply a question: when the members of your staff ask you what to do, turn it around and ask them what *they* think. As the people closest to the front lines, they know the answer. Help them become better leaders, and you won't need all those meetings.

To develop my potential, I have to develop my people.

"Greatness does not depend on the size of your command, but on the way you exercise it."

—Marshall Koch

In World War II, the German Panzer tanks were precision-built, highly engineered, and well-oiled fighting machines that could easily outmaneuver the loosely engineered, clanking, ill-fitted Soviet tanks. The Germans were expected to easily overrun the Russian position. But in the subzero weather of the steppes, the oil in the tightly engineered panzers froze and bound them up, whereas the greater tolerances in the Soviet tanks' mechanical systems enabled them to continue running and rout the Germans.

Reflections:

To perform at our best under pressure, we have to be loose and relaxed. As managers, we have to tolerate the idiosyncratic behavior of our staff and allow them the flexibility to improvise as a fast-changing, high-stress situation develops. Too much control can bind up the operation and stop careers dead in their tracks.

I have to allow my staff members freedom to act on their own.

"You can't attack a problem while sitting in a foxhole."

—Bob Larrañaga

One of your great strengths as a workaholic is your willingness to take charge. But if you're not careful, your need to command can lead to pitched battles with your own superiors. Given an assignment, you may hit on an approach you like; then dig in and refuse to change your position if your boss disagrees. Like the soldiers in World War II, who believed bomb craters made the best foxholes, you are about to catch flak.

Reflections:

Since your management style is direct and forceful, when you encounter opposition, your tendency is to become argumentative. In an effort to prove your point, you may overreach and get lost in an obscure, convoluted line of reasoning that weakens your credibility. Suddenly the focus shifts from the problem itself to your line of reasoning. When that happens, you'd better duck, because the battle has become a contest of wills in which you are outgunned. At times like this, the best defense is a disarming sense of humor.

I'm going to be more flexible and follow the chain of command.

JANUARY 25

*"The executive exists to make sensible
exceptions to general rules."*
—Elting E. Morison

All of us struggle with control in our own way.
For you, it may be dealing with a chronically late
employee, or one who makes many personal phone
calls at work. It may be a question of dress codes or
absenteeism. Effective managers control results by
setting firm performance standards and by holding
people accountable. Ineffective managers are lax in
enforcing their standards, and exceptions become
the rule. Their vacillation is seen as "favoritism,"
and weakens morale and productivity.

Reflections:

When you set performance standards, nearly
everyone expects to be an exception to the rule. To
their way of thinking, it's "only fair"; but what's fair
to one may seem unfair to others. As a workaholic,
you may struggle with the question of "fair play."
After all, you haven't given yourself a fair shake
when it comes to work; so it's just possible you are
hard on your co-workers, too. Confused, you may
make too many exceptions. The next time you're
asked to do "the only fair thing," ask yourself if
you're trying to control results or events.

*To be effective, I should control results rather than
events.*

"Most people like hard work. Particularly when they are paying for it."
—Franklin P. Jones

The stick and carrot approach to employee motivation favored by workaholics is just one of several ways to increase productivity. The best way to improve performance is to simply measure it. That's what Western Electric discovered back in 1921 at its Hawthorne plant outside of Chicago. They tested the effect of different lighting levels on productivity and discovered performance improved no matter what level the lights were set at! Why?—because the workers knew their performance was being monitored.

Reflections:

In your need to exert control you may threaten, demand, cajole, and reward employees to improve their performance. But the easiest way to motivate them is by showing a genuine interest in them and their work. The time spent with them will not only improve productivity, but also morale.

I'm going to pay compliments as well as cash.

"Of all men's miseries, the bitterest is this, to know so much and to have control over nothing."

—Herodotus

One of the ways you may be inclined to exert control is by restricting the flow of information in your company or department. Keeping secrets is a way of maintaining power; no one can challenge or dispute facts that only you know for sure. But in the absence of hard facts, the rumors are apt to circulate throughout the company and you won't be able to control them. In an atmosphere of intrigue, your decisions may be misinterpreted, leading to morale problems, employee turnover and low productivity.

Reflections:

Only you can decide which information is confidential and which you can share. But it makes good business sense to share your vision for the company and the highlights of your business plan. You may also want to share monthly progress reports to build *ésprit de corps*. The more you're willing to share, the stronger the bonds of loyalty between your company and your employees.

I'm going to share my business plan with the staff.

*"Every man with an idea has at least two
or three followers."*
—Brooks Atkinson

If you would be a leader within your company,
you must master the art of articulating your goals in
such a way that they are not only clear but also in-
candescent. Avoid reliance on intimidation and
threats to control others. Use imagery, metaphor,
and analogy to transmit a vivid mental picture of
your goals. Cite case histories, point to role models,
and breathe new life into the facts and figures at
your disposal. It's not enough to communicate—you
must illuminate.

Reflections:

The acceptance of an idea is seldom based only
on that idea's merits. Many a good idea has been
squelched simply because no one championed it
with the fervor and commitment needed to ignite
the imaginations of his or her co-workers. Enthusiasm sells, but persistence closes the sale. You must
believe so intensely in what you're doing that others
are caught up in your excitement and resistance is
swept away. Your own enthusiasm will be a direct
result of your ability to illuminate your goals. You
have to see yourself succeeding.

I need to visualize my ideas for myself and others.

"I never issue orders."

—Alfred P. Sloan

Alfred Sloan, the second president of General Motors and father of the modern corporation, was not a controlling personality. He delegated both responsibility and authority. He knew that the art of delegation lies in saying *exactly* what results you want, not how to achieve them. He made suggestions and requests rather than giving orders. To make sure the assignment was understood, he asked to have his directions restated, he invited questions, and he asked questions in return. Then he provided the resources needed for the task and measured the results.

Reflections:

Workaholics often have vague, unrealistic goals. We define jobs loosely and expect everyone to do "whatever it takes" to get things done. As a result, no one knows what's expected from day to day, and we're forced to control too much. Are your goals well defined and communicated to your staff? Does your staff have the resources needed? Are job descriptions clear? Does the organization chart define channels of authority and communication? Do you measure performance or conformance?

Giving too many orders is a sure sign that I'm out of order.

"Choose a job you love, and you will never have to work a day in your life."
—Confucius

Why is it that some executives cope better with the stress and strain of their jobs than others? They seem to thrive on the challenges posed by their work; they're energized by their problems; they inspire those around them to excel. A study conducted by the University of Chicago among middle- and upper-level managers found that stress could be neutralized by psychological "hardiness." Hardiness consists of commitment to your work, a sense of mission and belonging, control over your actions, and a belief that change is normal and exciting.

Reflections:

The encouraging news in these findings is that hardiness is largely a matter of attitude. You can choose to renew your commitment to work. You can make an effort to belong and help the company fulfill its mission statement. You can accept the fact that all control is provisional and subject to change. Once you accept change as inevitable and exciting, it becomes a chance to grow.

I'm going to make a list of the things I enjoy about my job.

"Interruptions are an executive's work."
—Bob Larrañaga

Every executive is caught in the same time bind: the higher up the corporation you move, the longer the time span affected by your decisions, yet the less time you have to make those decisions. At the start of your career, your planning horizon may have been one day, one week, or one month. Your job was routine, and you had plenty of time to formulate plans. But now that your plans span one to five years, you have very little time for thoughtful reflection. At least twenty times a day, someone interrupts your thinking. You don't even control your own thoughts.

Reflections:

With every shift in thinking, there is an emotional release, a feeling of power and excitement, a surge of adrenalin that is exciting, stimulating, and addictive. But this feeling gradually subsides as you develop a "tolerance" for adrenalin. It takes more and more crises to put you in touch with your feelings. You start to make snap decisions and rush heedlessly from one crisis to the next looking for an adrenalin fix. You crave the interruptions, and the giddy sense that things are out of control and only you can set them aright.

The best way to fix a problem is calmly.

HOW TO DEAL WITH YOUR ENEMIES

In today's Gospel, regular temple goers and the learned are angry with Jesus. They are angry because he sits down at table with bad people, dirty people, disobedient, careless, stupid, faithless people, people who never come to worship or do the right things. Here they are, the good people, clean, law-abiding, well-washed, learned, faithful, and Jesus treats them as equals to the town scum. The good people are outraged. But that is what Jesus taught about the Kingdom of God. Everybody belongs to the Kingdom. Love means forgiveness. In the course of living, we are often hurt or offended by others. Holding on to these hurts over months or years is stressful and can cause minor and major diseases. Learning to forgive significant hurts and then move on is an important part of being healthy in both mind, body and spirit. That's how Jesus tells his followers to deal with their enemies. Forgive them seven times seventy times, because we are all members of the Kingdom of God.

**SPIRIT AND HEALTH BULLETIN
SAINT MARY OF NAZARETH
HOSPITAL CENTER**

Mak

*A support grou
affected by*

For More

Hea
(70

FEBRUARY

Trust

Our need for control makes us guarded
and suspicious of others. We're slow to
trust. As a result, we do not share information freely, nor delegate effectively;
and as a result we are chronically overworked. To restore sanity to our lives,
we must turn our will over to God.
Only after we have placed our trust in a
Higher Power can we learn to trust
others.

FEBRUARY 1

"Trust your hopes, not your fears."
—David Mahoney

During the time of the Roman empire, many statues had interchangeable heads so that the monuments might better portray the shifting fortunes of the heads of state. In the corridors of today's power elite, the nameplates on the doors are interchangeable. Since 1981, the heads of company after company, and department after department, have lost their jobs. Over 25 million positions were eliminated by Fortune 500 companies. Many who still have jobs don't know whether to trust their hopes or their fears. They live in dread of the day when all their hard work may prove to have been in vain.

Reflections:

When times get tough, we workaholics bear down on ourselves and our staffs. As the pressure continues to build, we may become rigid, demanding, and mistrustful. In a crisis, we may threaten and blame others, relying on intimidation rather than inspiration, but our behavior is self-defeating because it undermines trust at a time when we most need to be trusted. In difficult times, try to keep your head and rely on your staff. Share with them an encouraging word, a smile, or a joke.

I have to keep my head when all the people about me are losing theirs.

*"Knowledge is power, but enthusiasm is
the spark."*

—Bob Larrañaga

You can spend your entire career trying to out-smart the other guy and earn a corner office with a panoramic view. But the truth is you can't do it on your own. Much of your success depends on how well you delegate. There are plenty of people who have the facts and figures at their command, and nothing more, because they lack the ability to work through others. True leaders not only have faith in themselves, but others, as well. Their trust breeds enthusiasm and inspires others to live up to their expectations.

Reflections:

Trust is a habit you can develop by delegating more to others, starting with the person you rely on most often, your secretary. Instead of hovering over her while she's typing and pointing out errors, give her a chance to proofread; better yet, give her a chance to compose simple letters for you. Ask her to manage your appointment calendar; let her over-see the departmental budget for clerical supplies. As your trust in her grows and her performance improves, you'll naturally find it easier to trust others as well.

My power grows as I share it with others.

FEBRUARY 3

"Wise sayings often fall on barren ground; but a kind word is never thrown away."

—Sir Arthur Helpe

If you ask Mary Kay Ash, founder of Mary Kay Cosmetics, the secret of her success, she simply says, "The Golden Rule—treating others as you'd want to be treated." The incredible growth of her business from a five hundred-square foot storefront to a multi-million corporation rests squarely on Mary Kay's unshakable faith in the people she considers her company's most valuable asset. You have to make them feel important, recognize their achievements, and, as she says, "Praise them to success."

Reflections:

The hallmark of the Mary Kay Cosmetics' motivation program is consistent, conspicuous recognition of the sales associates. However, there is a difference between praise and encouragement. The praiser says, "I'm proud of you," whereas the encourager says, "You must feel great." The encourager builds self-esteem from within. How long has it been since you built the self-esteem of one of your subordinates? Is there someone whose confidence needs bolstering? A word from you right now may be all it takes.

I'm going to praise my employees to success.

FEBRUARY 4

"Language was given to man to conceal thought."

—Talleyrand

At the outset of our careers, we're trained to think with a pencil in our hand and told that we haven't thought it out until we've written it out. Although that may be true, we workaholics overdo everything, including memo writing. We spend an hour at night writing a memo rather than taking five minutes during the day to tell someone what's on our mind. We make five photocopies when three would do. And we bury ourselves in paperwork because we don't trust the spoken word.

Reflections:

The average memo takes fifty-four minutes for planning, composing and editing. Routine documents are rewritten 4.2 times before they reach their intended audience. If you want to cut down on your paperwork, write fewer memos. Talk to your co-workers in person or by phone. Reply to someone else's memo by jotting your answer on the original. Create form letters for answering routine correspondence, and if you must write, use dictation when possible.

Before writing a memo, I'll ask myself if I can communicate the same idea faster and better in person.

FEBRUARY 5

*"We have too many high sounding
words, and too few actions that corre-
spond with them."*

—Abigail Adams

A natural skepticism makes workaholics wary
of verbal communication. We prefer to "put it in
writing." But management by memo has limitations.
First, it is expensive; the average memo costs
$106.15 to write, and, in fact, many companies
spend as much on their copier machines as on their
telephones. Second, the sheer volume of paperwork
slows down decisionmaking. And, finally, memos
simply cannot substitute for one-on-one discussions.
Eavin Shames, of General Foods, put it this way:
"Memos just don't move the heart and soul."

Reflections:

If you want to get on top of your paperwork,
clean out your files and "when in doubt, toss it out."
Follow time management expert Alan Lakein's paperwork rule: handle each piece of paper only once.
And, as for your memo writing—if you send your
staff more memos than they send you, the chain of
command has broken down, and they have delegated their work to you. Get out from behind your desk,
and find out what they are really doing.

*An empty wastebasket is the sign of a cluttered
mind. Today I will clean out my files.*

"Doubt isn't the opposite of faith; it's an element of faith."
—Paul Tillich

In every organization, the mail stream flows toward the source of power; those that control the flow of information, hold the power. We workaholics sense this and often develop an encyclopedic knowledge of our businesses. But our knowledge is primarily secondhand information, delivered by the mailperson, after others have developed the ideas, assembled the facts, and presented them in an organized manner. There is no convenient, firsthand way to verify everything we need to know; in other words, much of our knowledge is based on trust. And the higher up the corporate ladder we go, the more we must trust.

Reflections:

You'll probably read several magazines each week to stay abreast of your field, plus numerous other newsweeklies and business journals. Reading consumes much of your time. Yet competing trade journals overlap in their coverage of hard news by as much as 60 percent. Why not read alternate issues of competing magazines and trust your staff to bring anything you miss to your attention? You'll spend less time reading and more time thinking.

Ultimately, all truths rest on faith. It's only a question of whom I believe.

"Success is simply a matter of luck. Ask any failure."

—Earl Wilson

Those who can't delegate freely, are inevitably caught in a Tar Baby Trap. In *Tales of the Old South*, when Brer Rabbit found the Tar Baby by the side of the road, his curiosity got the best of him. He poked at the Tar Baby to see if it would move, but his hand got caught. Naturally, he tried to free himself, but his other hand stuck, too. So he jumped in with both feet; and before he knew it, he was completely trapped. If you're not careful which problems you poke at, you can get stuck, too. Save your curiosity for the thornier problems.

Reflections:

The story of the Tar Baby has a happy—and, for workaholics—instructive ending. You see, Brer Rabbit stopped wrestling with his problem and started using his head. He talked Brer Fox and Brer Bear into throwing him into the briar patch. Now, to anyone else that would have been an even thornier predicament—but not to Brer Rabbit, who was born in the briar patch. The fact is, we're all good at solving some problems and delegating the rest. Don't poke your head into someone else's problem without knowing what you're getting into.

I have enough problems without poking into someone else's.

*"One of the greatest labor-saving devices
is trust."*

—Bob Larrañaga

In most offices, the in-box on the mail tray is located on top and the out-box is located on the bottom. It's almost as if, in positioning the trays, we're saying that there is no ceiling on how much work we are willing to take on, though there is definitely a limit to how much we can put out. The only way you can manage your workload is to balance the inflow and outflow through delegation. Why not switch the position of your mail trays and start trusting others to help you manage the work?

Reflections:

If you're looking for a way to lighten your workload and motivate others, try trusting them. There's no better way to let your co-workers know you believe in them than to assign them a difficult task, spell out the details of the activity and hold them accountable for the results. Check back with them often, however, to make sure they are progressing as scheduled, and offer an encouraging word of advice or praise whenever they need it.

An encouraging word from me can get others to trust in themselves.

FEBRUARY 9

"I could no more give this up than an alcoholic could give up his whiskey."
—Ted Turner III

Entrepreneur Ted Turner inherited his family's near-bankrupt outdoor billboard company at age twenty one, when his father died of alcoholism. Through daring and self-reliance, Turner created a multibillion-dollar media sports enterprise and became a swashbuckling workaholic. Like Ted Turner, other workaholics are survivors. During the formative stages of our careers, many of us experienced a crisis in which we felt abandoned or betrayed. It may have been a ruthless boss or a back-stabbing co-worker, but we survived and resolved to never again trust others completely.

Reflections:

The price we pay for self-reliance is a sense of isolation, which adds to our work load and stress. It seems as if there is no one we can trust with our problems. This sense of loneliness is strongest at work, where the hierarchial structure makes it difficult to form personal relationships. But it also affects our family life and social life. Many workaholics have difficulty forming close personal relationships. What about you?

I have to be strong enough to be vulnerable.

FEBRUARY 10

"Good management consists of showing average people how to do the work of superior people."
—John D. Rockefeller

"But you know this project better than I do . . ." "Can you give us a hand . . ." "The client expects you to be involved . . ." Sound familiar? When you adopt a new management style, co-workers will still expect you to take charge and do everything yourself. They're accustomed to delegating work back to you and may resent the extra work load at first. It's flattering to feel needed and only natural to respond when someone needs help, but the best response may be a word of encouragement.

Reflections:

You have to replace your self-reliant style with a new, more trusting management approach. In delegating, be explicit about your expectations, and allow others the freedom to do the job their way. If you're not sure they can handle the complete project, delegate by degrees: break the project into discreet steps, and assign simpler tasks at first. Be sure to recognize those who do good work. As your trust level grows, delegate more complex tasks and, eventually the entire project. One of your great satisfactions as a manager will be helping others grow.

Life is a do-it-yourself project.

FEBRUARY 11

*"If it's obvious what you have to do, you
are not getting proper input."*
—James E. McCormick

As the publisher of the *Washington Post*, Katherine Graham is the highest salaried and arguably the most influential woman in the country. Yet she came to her position ill prepared when the untimely death of her husband forced her to assume management of the family newspaper. A middle-aged housewife, Graham had to win the respect of everyone from senior editors to press operators and circulation managers. But with the help of trusted advisers she was able to get the proper input, and quickly proved herself a strong leader.

Reflections:

Under Katherine Graham, the Washington Post Company became a media empire, and her employees eventually dubbed her Katherine the Great. She instinctively grasped the importance of surrounding herself with people who were experts in their specialties. Then she delegated both the responsibility and the authority for achieving her goals. Are you able to delegate completely and confidently, or do you practice management by meddling?

No one can prove to me that he or she is trustworthy unless I take a chance.

> *"The biggest burden a growing company faces is having a full-blooded entrepreneur as its owner."*
>
> —Derek du Toit

Many entrepreneurs become workaholics because they can't relax, let down their guard, and enjoy their success. They fear being victimized by events beyond their control. Their defensiveness makes them quick to deny responsibility when things go wrong. As a result, they may be surrounded by sycophants and political infighters. When these gamespeople manage a project, it usually goes through six stages: enthusiasm, disillusionment, panic, search for the guilty, punishment of the innocent, and honor to the nonparticipants. In the end, everyone becomes cynical and cautious.

Reflections:

To be an outstanding manager, you have to accept responsibility for your actions *and* those of your staff. You must hold yourself accountable for your failure to delegate properly and supervise effectively. If your staff members do not meet your expectations, first examine your role and then examine theirs. By accepting responsibility, you will earn their trust.

My duty as a manager is to shoulder responsibility for my staff's performance.

> "An intelligent man knows when the wrong answer has been given; a creative man knows when the wrong question has been asked."
>
> —Anton Jay

There is a streak of skepticism in every workaholic: we always question, always doubt and hesitate to trust anyone, or anything at face value. Our skepticism multiplies at RAM speed when we gain access to a personal computer. Suddenly we can challenge any assumption by asking the computer, "What if . . . ?" and by watching it churn out answers. Given this power, it's easy to lose sight of the fact that real breakthroughs occur when someone dares to challenge the trends and ask, "Why not?"

Reflections:

The role of expert is one every workaholic enjoys. Whether we use a computer or not, we delight in outthinking and second-guessing co-workers. We have little patience for questions that can't be answered with hard facts. By contrast, creative managers excel at finding problems rather than solutions. They're quick to ask, "Why not?" Once they identify a problem, they delegate the search for a solution to more methodical, analytical thinkers so that they themselves can keep an open mind.

I have to be more trusting of my co-workers.

"Executive ability is deciding quickly and getting somebody else to do the work."

—J. G. Pollard

Given the turnover rate in most companies, a supervisor of twelve people has to fill another position every three months or so. If you don't have a backup candidate lined up, it can take six weeks to find someone you trust. Meanwhile you're juggling an increased work load and trying to find time to schedule interviews. The added responsibilities can increase your stress and lead to a bad hiring decision, so that the cycle never ends.

Reflections:

As a workaholic, you're probably more oriented toward tasks, than toward people. So you're likely to devote your peak energy period each day to handling the heavy task load you now face. Personnel interviews are most likely scheduled for late in the day—when you have the time. But after 5:00 p.m., your energy level drops, your attention span shortens, and your judgment fades. Tired and hungry, you're inclined to rush through the interview and overlook important details. To make better, faster hiring decisions, schedule interviews for periods when you're at your best. There is no harder job than hiring.

Recruiting top-quality people is my number one job.

"If you insist on hiring executives below you in stature, you will soon find yourself running a pygmy business."
—David Ogilvy

Andrew Carnegie, one of the wealthiest men in history, had a special gift for recruiting talented executives. At the peak of his success, when asked to name his greatest asset, he said, "Take away all our factories, our trades, our avenues of transportation, our money; but leave me our organization, and in four years, I will have reestablished myself." The secret to Carnegie's success was best expressed in the words engraved on his tomb: "Here lies a man whose special gift was the ability to convince men of greater talent to work for him." Are you big enough to hire someone more able than you are?

Reflections:

The recruitment process poses a quandary for workaholics. On the one hand, we want to surround ourselves with other workaholics who share our ambition and relentless drive. On the other hand, we are reluctant to trust another pencil-chomping, fire-breathing workaholic. The danger is that we will recruit people who don't threaten us, simply because they have less talent or experience. In the end, we may be surrounded by mediocrities who excel at political infighting.

I have to be big enough to hire people bigger than I am.

> *"When the character of a man is not clear to you, look at his friends."*
> —Japanese proverb

He was hunchbacked, had failing eyesight, wore rumpled, ill-fitting suits, smoked foul-smelling cigars, and was an irascible codger. By today's standards, he was virtually unemployable. Yet Charles Steinmetz stood as a colossus astride the world of science and computers. Without him, Bell Labs could not have achieved its preeminent position. If Steinmetz, or someone like him, applied to you for a job, would you trust him in a responsible position?

Reflections:

The ultimate test of a manager is the ability to recognize and recruit gifted people. Each of us is naturally attracted to people just like us, but that is not always wise. As workaholics, we're apt to hire someone who can "do it all," hard-working generalists like ourselves. We are inevitably disappointed, because Superworker doesn't exist. Before recruiting, determine your strengths and weaknesses, admit you can't do it all, and find specialists to fill in your gaps. The best and brightest tend to be highly focused specialists like Steinmetz.

To achieve my true potential, I have to recognize my limitations.

FEBRUARY 17

"The man who questions opinions is wise; the man who quarrels with facts is a fool."

—Frank A. Garbrett

Does it pay to give someone the benefit of the doubt? When the cold, uncaring logic of a computer decides the issue, the answer is yes. In a computer simulation at Rand Corporation, two players competed in a non-zero-sum game called the Prisoner's Dilemma. Each player had to decide whether to squeal on his or her accomplice or hold to his or her alibi. The best strategy, called "Tit for Tat," gives the accomplice benefit of the doubt until proven wrong. In "Tit for Tat," you don't try to beat the other player; you reciprocate, but both players therefore win.

Reflections:

If trusting others makes sense to a computer, why do we have so much trouble seeing it? Unlike the computer's "thought," our thinking is colored by emotion and imagination. We fear the consequences of delegation and exaggerate the risks of losing control. In so doing, we overlook the fact that failure to trust limits our effectiveness. We become prisoners of our own dilemma.

Trusting others involves some risk, but the greater risk lies in not trusting them.

FEBRUARY 18

"Problems are the price of progress."
—Branch Rickey

All change is experienced as a loss. We simply do not trust the unknown. Take, for example, the manager who has just been promoted—clearly a change for the better. Yet many managers, when promoted, feel a sense of personal inadequacy and fear failure. They actually miss their former positions and the feeling of mastery and control that they had. The danger is that they will not relinquish their former duties, but will compete with their subordinates and thus ultimately fail in their new roles.

Reflections:

As a workaholic, your need for order and stability makes you wary and guarded in a new, unfamiliar role. On the one hand, you felt comfortable in your old job; you knew you could do it better than anyone else (why else would they have promoted you!); and on the other hand you just don't trust your replacement, right? Nonetheless, your future success depends, in large part, on your ability to delegate. You must give your subordinates clear directions and the responsibility and authority to carry out their tasks, monitoring and controlling the results.

In order to be trusted, I must trust.

FEBRUARY 19

"There is more to every job than working."

—Anonymous

At the end of World War II, Faber, Germany, was the pencil capital of Europe. To protect its virtual monopoly, the Eberhard Faber Company was highly secretive about its manufacturing processes. But that didn't stop Armand Hammer, a U.S. businessman who had obtained rights to manufacture pencils in the Soviet Union, as part of that nation's literacy program. Hammer built an exact replica of the German town deep inside the Soviet Union, toured the site with several Faber craftsmen, and offered them huge bonuses for joining him. In less than a year, the factory was operational; inside five years, it exported pencils worldwide.

Reflections:

Hammer's genius lay in recognizing that his real obstacle was not only the Eberhard Faber Company, but also its corporate culture. Every company is a community with a culture all its own. The culture includes unwritten norms, informal activities, and customs binding the employees to it. Office parties, picnics, bowling, and softball teams may seem tangential to the purpose of the business, but they foster a sense of community that is essential. They are a positive sign that employees enjoy working together.

Today I'm going to join one of the company's teams.

> *"Those who are fond of setting things to right have no great objection to setting them to wrong."*
> —William Hazlett

Where are you on the company's organization chart?—not the official chart published by management, but the invisible one circulated by word of mouth during coffee breaks, at the vending machines, and in the corridors. Every company has an invisible infrastructure, with its own chain of command, a hidden hierarchy, or "in-group," made up of people who are loyal to peers rather than to management. They don't trust management.

Reflections:

There is a negative bias in many corporate cultures because the members of the hidden hierarchy are wary of management and convinced that they can do a better job of running the company. They may even undermine management initiatives ("We tried that before"; "That's not the way it's done around here"). Their performance norms are not public and are seldom voiced for all to hear and question. It's up to you to challenge the "in-group" and show where your loyalty belongs.

My first loyalty is to the company.

"Some folks can look so busy doing nothin' that they seem indispensable."
—Kin Hubbard

Many a workaholic has an unwitting accomplice, another employee who is "busy doing nothing" and whose poor performance seems to justify all the workaholic's extra efforts. Never mind that we might have worked just as hard anyway, we feel as though we're being used. Right or wrong, the other person becomes the focal point for all our frustrations about work. Gradually, we withdraw our support, become aloof and demeaning. We may still do extra work for that person, but in reality we are uncooperative.

Reflections:

Has a co-worker slackened off on the job, leaving you to shoulder a heavier work load? Or have you simply made someone else a scapegoat for your own workaholic behavior? If you're certain the problem stems from someone else's performance, why stifle your feelings? Your resentment may increase, along with the work load pressures, until a minor incident triggers an angry outburst out of all proportion to the cause. Before you appear unpredictable and mercurial and your reputation suffers, discuss the work load problem with the other person.

My goal for today is to talk myself out of at least one job.

"Treat people as if they were what they ought to be, and you help them become what they are capable of being."
—Johann Wolfgang von Goethe

Does the very thought of conducting a personnel review tie you up in knots? If so, you're not alone. Most executives are uncomfortable candidly discussing another employee's performance. Our apprehension increases sharply if we expect such employees to deny, deflect, defend, or counterattack. Our carefully rehearsed remarks can quickly become critical if they challenge our appraisal. We may belittle their efforts, run down their motives, and rob them of their dignity.

Reflections:

With someone's future at stake, you can't afford to improvise in a personnel review. Give the other person several days' notice, so he or she is not surprised and defensive. Ask the person to review the job description, rate his or her performance, and come prepared to discuss "progress." Hold the review in private, and allow the other person to speak first. Focus on the job description and other measurable yardsticks. End by saying what you expect, and hold him or her to it.

Every personnel review is a chance for me to reaffirm someone.

FEBRUARY 23

"Discussion is an exchange of knowledge; argument, an exchange of ignorance."

—Robert Quillen

A study conducted for the American Management Association showed that lack of feedback ranks fourth among causes of job-related stress. Workaholics have difficulty giving subordinates appropriate feedback. When we encounter a problem employee, our natural reaction is a quick burst of anger. If the problem persists, we avoid the other person and resort to management by memo, or leave Post-it notes all over his or her chair. This cuts off dialogue and leaves the employee frustrated, angry, and distrustful of us.

Reflections:

If you find yourself sending an employee one disciplinary memo after another, it's time for a frank and open discussion. Hold the meeting in a neutral setting, away from phones and other interruptions. Bring any pertinent documentation and, at the outset, review the file; then ask for an explanation. Share how you feel about the problem, state your expectations, and make clear what will happen if the situation doesn't improve. No one benefits when you avoid dealing with a problem.

I'm going to deal openly with disciplinary problems.

FEBRUARY 24

*"O Lord, please fill my mouth with
worthwhile stuff, and nudge me when
I've said enough."*

—Anonymous

Do you have a tendency to talk *at* people instead of *with* them? Some workaholics monopolize the conversation and challenge other points of view, occasionally belittling other people or cutting them off. By contrast, effective managers spend 60 to 80 percent of their day in exchanges with their staff members. They excel at giving and receiving feedback. According to *Fortune* magazine, the effective leader "need not be charismatic. What may work best is a willingness to *listen* and learn bordering on self-effacement."

Reflections:

Researchers at the University of Minnesota attribute nearly 60 percent of business misunderstandings to poor listening. A good listener asks open-ended questions and takes notes. Notes visualize the other person's idea—83 to 87 percent of what we learn comes through our eyes. Note-taking also slows your mind down—otherwise your thoughts may wander because we think four times faster than speak. Finally, notes let you repeat and clarify what the other person said.

To listen better, I must take more notes.

FEBRUARY 25

*"More appealing than knowledge itself
is the feelings of knowing."*
—Daniel Boorstin

Sharp words. Wounding words. Snub-nosed,
full-metal-jacketed words. We speak in machine gun
bursts, fire off catchphrases, and use clipped clichés
to squelch any disagreement. We end our sentences
with words like "Right?" as if we were interested in
a response—but we're not really looking for feedback. We expect the other person to nod (or duck),
because as far as we're concerned, we're right. Our
speech patterns give us away. We're workaholics.

Reflections:
A break in communications usually leads to a
breakdown in trust. One side thinks it has all the
answers and refuses to listen to what the other side
says. If you grab the first cliché that comes to mind
and you shoot from the lip, you won't communicate
effectively. Clichés are wornout metaphors or sim-
iles, and are not literally true. They're also general-
izations and, as such, open to misinterpretation.
They don't really say what you mean. At the same
time, a rapid-fire delivery prevents the other side
from answering, and as a result you don't get to hear
their viewpoint.

*I'm more likely to solve a problem when I approach
it from both sides.*

*"Opportunity is sometimes hard to rec-
ognize if you're only looking for a lucky
break."*

—Monta Crane

Ray Mithun, who carved out successful careers
in advertising and banking, compared his management role to that of a catfish in the fish market tank.
A catfish, Mithun would explain, is a bottom feeder,
stirring up food the other fish missed, bumping into
them, forcing them to rise up, move about, stay
healthy. Successful managers stir things up and
keep the staff moving, seeking opportunities others
missed, forcing them to rise to the occasion. Theirs
is a healthy form of skepticism and questioning of
the status quo.

Reflections:

One of your natural gifts is a restless, driving
desire to stir things up. It's one reason why people
enjoy working with you. But if you find someone
working less than 100 percent, you may assign them
meaningless busy work. This sort of purposeless activity saps energy and spirit. Actually, the most productive employees only work 85 percent of the time;
the rest is taken up with personal activities and minutiae. Like the fish in the tank, we all stop once in
a while to let the sand settle.

*I'm entitled to at least two coffee breaks a day, and
so is everyone who works for me.*

*"Delegating is the art of letting someone
else have your way."*

—Anonymous

Vince Lombardi, former coach of the Green Bay
Packers, was a masterful strategist, planning every
detail of every play in advance. But if the defense
changed formation at the line of scrimmage, he expected his quarterback to call an audible. The coach
had complete trust in his field general. They both
had the same goal in mind and differed only in how
to get there. Effective delegators focus on the ends
rather than means; they allow for individual work
styles. They know what Lombardi meant when he
said, "Life is a series of audibles."

Reflections:

For workaholics, trusting does not come easily.
Our need for control makes us mistrustful of any
change in the game plan. We may delegate responsibility, but not authority. How comfortable are you
in delegating? Have you accepted the fact that your
proper role is to set objectives, monitor performance, and measure results. It's up to those on the
scrimmage line to decide how the game will be
played. You have to trust them to reach your goals.

*I'm going to delegate authority as well as responsi-
bility.*

"He has exceeded my expectations and done even better."

—Yogi Berra

A study of several large companies showed that departments with the highest productivity had managers who praised performance once every hour, whereas departments with the lowest productivity had managers who praised performance once a day. We workaholics are slow to praise. We think the ultimate compliment is another challenging assignment; it's our way of saying we trust an employee. Work without praise soon becomes drudgery, and productivity plummets if employees learn that the reward for hard work is more hard work.

Reflections:

There are only two ways to improve the performance of your staff: training and motivation. Training is standardized by function within a company, but motivation is highly individualized and requires all your interpersonal skills. Some people seek self-actualization by accepting challenges, but far more are motivated by money. Others seek recognition. Still others must feel accepted as a member of the management team, and so on. To delegate effectively, know what motivates each of your co-workers.

Anyone who works for money alone is underpaid. Today I'll pay each co-worker a compliment.

"I think we may safely trust a good deal
more than we do."
—Henry David Thoreau

One of the most pivotal passages of the New
Testament occurred when Peter, standing in the
courtyard, denied that he knew Jesus. The future of
Christianity was decided by what happened next—
in the silent exchange between Jesus and the man
he had trusted to lead his church. Had Christ turned
away and rejected Peter, the story might have ended
differently. But in all likelihood Christ winced at the
words he knew were coming and turned to Peter—
not with the look of "I told you so"—but with the
tearful look of forgiveness.

Reflections:

How do you react when people let you down?
If you're like most workaholics, you are reluctant to
give anyone a second chance. Once disappointed,
you hesitate to trust the person again. But when you
stop to think about it, there have been many times
someone else gave you a second chance to prove
yourself. Remember the first proposal you wrote and
the first presentation you gave?—how unsteady and
unsure you felt? Had it not been for the trust and
encouragement of a boss who believed in you, you
might not be where you are today.

It's time I gave others a second chance.

MARCH

Time

Overwhelmed by our work, we are unable to establish priorities and try to do two and three things at once. But although we are efficient, we are not effective. Our Higher Power must become the first priority in our lives before we can decide what else is important to us. Only then can we truly manage our time.

MARCH 1

"And in today already walks tomorrow."
—Samuel Taylor Coleridge

The alarm clock stirs at 5:30 a.m., and you roll over in bed to see a shaft of light clear your windowsill: dawn, the most inspiring moment of the day. The rising sun lifts your spirits with the promise of a new beginning, a chance to start over, refreshed and renewed. No matter what happened yesterday, it's behind you now, forever in the past. If you made a mistake, if you lost a sale, or a key employee resigned, if you failed to meet your own expectations, it's history now and the rest of your life lies ahead.

Reflections:

Those first faint rays of sunlight that crossed your windowsill took over eight minutes to reach you, traveling at 186,000 miles a second. By the time you received the sun's "wake-up call" and threw off your blankets, the day was nearly nine minutes old. Would you like to have those nine minutes back? Simply set your wristwatch ahead. You'll give yourself a margin of error between appointments, and some quiet time to collect your thoughts during the day. Nine minutes a day may not seem like much, but over the course of a year, it adds up to more than two extra days—make that holidays!

I'm going to set my watch ahead nine minutes.

MARCH 2

"Time is a very precious gift of God; so precious that it is only given to us moment by moment."

—Amelia Barr

The alarm clock next to your bed not only tells the hour, but also says something about our changing attitudes toward time. The graceful, sweeping hands of the clock have been replaced by a disjointed LED numeric display that says time is no longer a continuum, but discrete, fragmented, abbreviated flashes of reality. Yes, you can hit the snooze button and listen to subliminal motivation tapes while your morning coffee brews in the percolator plugged into the clock's auxiliary jack. You *can* do three things at once, but why?

Reflections:

Our compulsion to squeeze more into each moment is so great that scientists now define one second as the time it takes for the microwaves of heated cesium to vibrate 83 million times. Left unchecked, our natural tendency is to squeeze more and more into each fleeting second. Isn't it time you woke up to what this compulsion is doing to you?

I'm going to set my radio alarm clock to a station that plays upbeat music so that I start my day in the right mood.

MARCH 3

"For fast-acting relief, try slowing down."

—Lily Tomlin

The lengthening shadows of spring gently remind us that the sun is an erratic timepiece, gaining as much as three minutes a day so that a full calendar year has an extra 5 hours, 48 minutes, and 46.9 seconds. Those extra hours and minutes add up over four years to the extra day in leap year. As measured by the sun, there is no such thing as "standard time." Do you suppose it's time you looked at your own standards to see if you're setting realistic deadlines for yourself?

Reflections:

To make every day count, take a flexible approach to scheduling your time. Time management experts recommend allowing 25 percent more time for each task than you expect to take. They also suggest that you schedule only half your time. If the work requires a great deal of concentration or is highly stressful, plan on a diversion periodically. Most people need a ten-minute break every hour. If you expect interruptions, set aside an access period each day when you can meet with others. In setting your own time-management standards, make them as flexible as nature's.

I'm going to take a ten-minute break every hour.

*"All we have is the past, 'pleasant' and
future."*
—Tim Hansel

The ancient Greeks marked time by a leisurely
lunar month that had no weeks. The Romans added
an eight-day week, but their calendar was eleven
days longer than the solar year. By 1330, the twenty
four-hour day and sixty-minute hour were in use,
and in 1477 the second hand appeared on clocks.
Finally, in 1582, Pope Gregory introduced the modern calendar. To make it coincide with the solar
year, the pope declared October 4 would be followed by October 15. Thousands complained they
had lost ten days' wages; others feared their lives
had been shortened; but they adopted the Gregorian
calendar, and the race against time began.

Reflections:

Today's atomic clocks measure time by the precise oscillation of electrons. Paradoxically, quantum
physics demonstrates that between measurements
the oscillating electron isn't anywhere: if you're not
measuring it, it simply is not there. So we have come
full circle: time is whatever we choose to measure—
a lunar month, an eight-day week, a sixty-minute
hour, or an electron. The next time you're running
behind schedule, do as Pope Gregory did—remove
a few dates from your calendar.

I need to be present to the present.

MARCH 5

"Living is entirely too time consuming."
—Irene Peters

In our culture, time is linear; but in other cultures, time is not so one-dimensional. The Tiv people of Nigeria keep track of time by what is being sold in the marketplace: leather day, brass day, cattle day, and so on. However, two adjacent villages might hold their markets on different days, so that yesterday is today and today is tomorrow in a never-ending Möbius strip of time. In the Hopi and Sioux languages, there is no past or future tense; it's as though everything were happening in the eternal now. The Eskimos in the Arctic Circle live outside the international time zones so that, for the inhabitants, our concept of time is irrelevant.

Reflections:

In reality, each of us lives in our own time zone. In your daily schedule, set aside blocks of personal time, especially during periods of peak work load. Allow enough time between appointments to review the files on your next project and compose your thoughts. In planning the day's events, allow 25 percent more time to complete each job than you think it will take.

Today I will review my calendar for the coming week.

MARCH 6

"Time is dead as long as it is being clicked off by little wheels; only when the clock stops does time come to life."
—William Faulkner

Daylight savings time. We take it for granted now, but it was only in 1966 that it became the law of the land, a semiannual reminder that time is whatever we say it is. We move the hands of our clocks forward and back, dutifully; and yet we persist in seeing time as some objective standard, rather than an arbitrary and fluid concept. We say, "Time waits for no man . . . ," and perpetuate the illusion that time stands beside us, scythe in hand.

Reflections:

We impatient workaholics see time as an adversary to be conquered and won over. But to the truly successful executives, time is an ally. They are so involved in their work that they enjoy every moment on the job. This patient attention to the task at hand is what accounts for many of their achievements. Nothing worthwhile can be achieved overnight. Greatness takes times.

There is no such thing as a quick fix.

MARCH 7

*"Don't look back. Somethin' might be
gaining on you."*

—Satchel Paige

It's possible to board a supersonic jet at 7:55 a.m. in Indianapolis and outrace the sun to Chicago, landing at 7:48 a.m. Central Standard Time. The plane arrives seven minutes before it left! But despite the flight attendant's cheery reminder to reset our watches, we cannot change our biorhythms. Like the tangs of a tuning fork, our bodies are attuned to nature's rhythms. Our heartbeat and pulse rate, our breathing out and in, our waking and sleeping, must synchronize with nature's timepiece, the sun.

Reflections:

One effective way to help develop a sense of pacing is to take a long, leisurely walk each day, leaving the portable radio behind, in order to tune into the sights and sounds of nature and your own thoughts and feelings. Walking releases in the brain endorphins, the body's own tranquilizers. It also stretches the legs and relaxes muscles in which tension has accumulated during the day. As an added bonus, moderate walking (three miles per hour) burns about 270 to 285 calories for the average adult.

To develop a better sense of pacing, I'll take daily walks.

MARCH 8

*"If you can fill the unforgiving minute
with sixty seconds worth of distance
run, yours is the earth and everything
that's in it."*

—Rudyard Kipling

Workaholics never stop running, in an effort to squeeze sixty five or seventy seconds out of every "unforgiving minute." At work, we have two phones ringing at once, appointments back to back, and lunch at our desks. At home, we write memos during Monday night football; read the paper while pedaling our Exercycles; and walk the dog to the sounds from a walkman radio. Whenever possible, we do two things at once, and still our project lists grow. This is especially true of entrepreneurs, who work twelve hours a day for themselves, so they won't have to work eight hours a day for someone else.

Reflections:

This evening and on the weekend, why not take off your watch and allow yourself to be paced by your natural sense of timing? You'll be surprised at how much longer the day seems and how many meaningful moments there are to pause and enjoy when you don't have one eye on the clock.

To make the most of every minute, I'll stop counting the seconds.

"Yesterday is a cancelled check; tomorrow is a promissory note; today is the only cash you have—so spend it wisely."
—Kay Lyons

According to psychologists, one of the last mental faculties we acquire is the ability to project ourselves beyond the limits of time. We learn to contemplate the past, present, and future, go beyond the current moment, and see time as the continuum Einstein envisioned. But we workaholics often focus on the past and future and ignore each precious, fleeting moment of the present.

Reflections:

The past, present, and future are bound together like the pages in an appointment book, saddle-stitched in the spine so that the front and back are one and the same. When an appointment book is laid open on a desk, the present is a two-page spread with yesterday and tomorrow having only one page each. So it should be with our own view of time. Flip through the pages of your appointment book to see if your schedule is as crowded now as it was a few months ago. Since these are the good old days we'll be talking about in the future, why not enjoy them now? Have you turned over a new leaf?

I'm going to take time each day for quiet reflection.

MARCH 10

"The trouble with life in the fast lane is that you get to the other end in an awful hurry."

—John Jensen

Recent surveys suggest that 70 percent of all executives are now workaholics, up from 50 percent only fifteen years ago. The ranks of workaholics are swollen with raw recruits who seized the new productivity tools: personal computers, answering machines, cellular phones, and faxes. With the new devices came an expectation of nonstop performance. You no longer have the two-day communication gap between sending and receiving messages. The responses arrive in nanoseconds until the sheer volume of information outstrips your ability to act on it.

Reflections:

Do you long for the good old days when business moved at the speed of paper and your biggest complaint was telephone tag and the paper chase? Take a closer look at one of the new productivity tools. With a phone modem, your personal computer can access electronic bulletin boards, which scan newswire services and trade and business journals to identify articles of predetermined interest. Bulletin boards can greatly reduce your reading time by providing you with your very own reader's digest.

I'm going to get a phone modem for our computer.

MARCH 11

"The present is a point just passed."
—David Russell

In the electronic village, we can fast forward, reverse, split-screen, dub, and zap our way right past the here and now with push-button speed. We can tune into the "golden oldies," watch a 1960s rerun, or program our videotape deck to record a future show for later viewing. We can record a letter on a dictating unit, replay messages on our telephone-answering machine, and retrieve messages in our electronic mailbox. We can span three time zones simultaneously in a teleconference. But can we connect with the present?

Reflections:

Timeshifting is so commonplace that *Esquire* magazine says, "There is no here here. There was no then then. There is no now now." The result is a dizzying, confusing state of affairs in which the only way to maintain your balance is by hitting the pause button long enough to meditate each day. Physically speaking, it takes only about 60 seconds for the nervous system to relax and another ten to twenty minutes to bring yourself back to equilibrium after a stressful day.

I'm going to give myself the gift of time.

MARCH 12

"Sleep fast. We need the pillows."
—Yiddish proverb

Management consultant Peter Drucker says time is the scarcest business resource: available in limited supply, it is inelastic, perishable, and unstorable. Still, there's the matter of those eight hours a night spent sleeping. As any workaholic knows, you can't get ahead wasting one-third of your life in bed! So we tell ourselves we don't need as much sleep as "normal" people and stretch our day beyond the limits of endurance, if not beyond the limits of time.

Reflections:

The Jewish and Muslim custom of beginning the day at sundown has a lot to recommend it in these days of frenetic, mind-numbing work. It's not so much that we need sleep to restore us physically, but rather that we need a psychological respite from the frenetic cares of the day. Some theorists believe that during sleep we sort out all the subconscious, peripheral thoughts that cross our mind during the day. Deprived of sleep, we become disoriented, paranoid, and may even hallucinate. Our problem-solving ability becomes impaired. Well rested, however, we handle our work efficiently, effectively, and calmly.

To be well rested I need at least six-and-a-half hours sleep.

MARCH 13

*"A committee—a group of men who keep
minutes and waste hours."*
—Fred Allen

A recent management survey showed that senior executives spend twenty three hours a week in meetings, not counting preparation time. Yet these same executives say only 58 percent of the meetings are effective, and 22 percent could have been handled with phone calls or memos. Obviously, meetings are one of the greatest consumers of your time, and anything you do to avoid them or manage them more efficiently can relieve your chronic sense of hurriedness.

Reflections:

To make the most of your meeting time, circulate an agenda in advance so that participants can gather backup material and prepare. Limit participation to those who must attend, set a time limit for the meeting, and appoint someone else to keep the minutes. Have your secretary keep your appointment calendar, in order to avoid playing telephone tag with people who want to set up meetings with you. Think twice before attending a meeting that can't begin until more chairs are brought into the room.

I need fewer committee meetings and more meetings of the mind.

"Time is the measure of business; as money is of wares."
—Francis Bacon

According to Robert Heller, the single most common managerial complaint is the inability to read more than a fraction of the printed material that crosses the executive's desks. Reading involves a tradeoff: as long as you are acquiring knowledge, you are not in a position to act on what you learn. But at some point, your learning curve levels off and your knowledge becomes abstract, speculative, and remote from day-to-day problems. You have to decide when to stop reading and when to start acting.

Reflections:

In reading, it's quality, not quantity, that counts. Procter & Gamble requires its managers to condense their proposals to a single page with exhibits attached, if necessary. 3M limits its proposals to no more than five pages. Many other companies require their proposals have an executive summary. Are your subordinates overwhelming you with needless minutiae?

I'm going to require my staff to write one-page memos or executive summaries on longer documents.

"If hard work were such a wonderful thing, surely the rich would have kept it all to themselves."
—Lane Kirkland

Long, hard hours of work are a rite of passage most newcomers go through in being initiated into a company. But when overtime becomes the norm; and you feel pressure to appear "busier than thou"; when your work begins to affect your mental, physical, or emotional well-being, then it's time to reassess your situation. As one senior executive said, "If you're putting in too many long hours, either you have too much to do, or you're not very good at it." Assuming you're good at your job, what can you do about the work load?

Reflections:

Try to stay on top of things and maintain a positive outlook by looking on the extra work as a chance to sharpen your skills. Keep track of how you're spending your time so you can make your case for help, if the work load continues unabated. A detailed time record should also help you schedule your work, because you'll have a good idea of how long each task takes. At the first sign of a business upturn, ask your boss for an assistant.

Things will work out as long as I keep a positive attitude.

*"There's never time to do it right.
There's always time to do it over."*
—Sign in workaholic's office

Without really thinking it through, many workaholics adopt the attitude of the watchmaker who was asked how he could sell his timepieces so cheaply. "Easy," he replied, "we make our profits repairing them." In our haste to succeed, we cut corners and sacrifice quality for quantity, hoping to catch our mistakes later. However, you can't inspect quality in afterward. You have to take the time to do it right the first time. You need good controls at every stage of production.

Reflections:

The underlying attitude of many workaholics is "Better never than late." But nothing of any lasting value can be created in haste. To improve the quality of our work, we have to develop a sense of pacing and an appreciation for process. We have to think through each step without getting carried away by our own enthusiastic plans. If you take the time to commit your plans to paper, the quality of your work will improve.

Shortcuts are usually a detour.

*"It's not true that life is one damn thing
after another—it's the same damn thing
over and over again."*
—Edna St. Vincent Millay

The average executive's work is interrupted once every twelve minutes. As we try to take in one problem after another, our emotions swing back and forth like a pendulum on a string. The greater our span of authority, the more problems we encounter and the wider our emotional swings become. Over a period of time, these emotional highs and lows have a cumulative effect on our nervous system. They take on a momentum of their own.

Reflections:

Once a pendulum is set in motion, the amount of time it takes to swing through its arc remains constant, despite the fact that the amplitude of each swing gradually diminishes. Something similar happens when our emotions sway through one crisis after another. Although the amplitude of our response diminishes with time, we go back and forth over the problems, again and again, late into the night, not letting go until the string plays out and we're emotionally and physically exhausted. To break the stress cycle, in the evening listen to soothing classical music.

Soothing, restful music can restore my inner harmony.

MARCH 18

*"I would not exchange my leisure hours
for all the wealth in the world."*
—Comte de Mirabeau

For over a hundred years, Big Ben has towered over Westminster Palace in London, the standard of time in an empire on which the sun never set. Its bell measures nine feet across, weighs thirteen-and-a-half tons, and can be heard for miles. Big Ben's pendulum has a tray on which stacks of old English pennies were once set to regulate the clock. The timekeeper would add a few pennies to slow it down or remove a few to speed things up. If only time could be purchased so cheaply!

Reflections:

If time is money, why do so few executives value their leisure time the same way they do their working hours? In business, you establish the value of your time by multiplying your base salary by three and dividing the sum by 1,750 working hours in a year. Using that same formula, if you earn $30,000, your weekend hours are each worth $51.43. If you earn $50,000, they're worth $85.72; and at that rate, next Saturday and Sunday are worth almost $1,300. How are you going to spend your valuable weekend time?

I'm going to spend my weekend just as I would any $1,300 expenditure.

MARCH 19

"Long-range planning does not deal with future decisions, but with the future of present decisions."
—Peter Drucker

Clock makers have known since the late 1600s, when Christian Huygens invented the pendulum, that if two clocks stand on the same support they gradually begin to oscillate in unison. This phenomenon, known as *entrainment*, also operates behind the scene in television tuners and in lasers, which emit waves of pulsating energy. Entrainment also affects the behavior of people working together in an office. The work flow develops a definite rhythm.

Reflections:

Do you get the feeling that you are often out of synchronization with the rest of your co-workers? Do you find yourself saying, "They don't know the time of day?" The fact that you are putting in longer hours, generating more paperwork, thinking up more projects than they can handle in a normal working day can create problems between you and your staff. It may actually disrupt the normal work rhythm and cause chaos and confusion. Why not ease up and get in rhythm with your staff?

If I want my job to run like clockwork, I have to be in rhythm with others.

> *"Doing well as a result of doing good.*
> *That's what capitalism is all about, isn't*
> *it?"*
>
> —Adnan M. Khashoggi

It's easy to say no to the dumb things, but how do you deal with reasonable demands on your time without appearing uncooperative? There is nothing wrong with saying no. It does not necessarily mean you're uncooperative. Your co-workers don't have the foggiest idea what's on your project list. So it's up to you to tell them when you're too busy. If you can help them, it's also reasonable for you to expect them to help on a project you have. You may be able to lighten one another's load.

Reflections:

In business, "what goes around, comes around"—if you help people, they'll help you, but only if you let them. Forget the self-reliant, do-it-yourself ways of a workaholic and ask for help. The next time someone interrupts what you're doing with a request for help, instead of saying yes or no, consider saying, "I'd be happy to help just as soon as I finish the project I'm working on now—maybe you can give me a hand." When you lend people a hand, they lend you theirs, too.

In reaching out to others, I must accept their hands, too.

"Hard work describes the amount more often than the difficulty."

—Anonymous

To some workaholics, success is not a matter of life and death—it's more important than that. In a Faustian bargain with time, they may not only sacrifice the quality of their own lives, but also that of loved ones. According to an article in *Psychology Today,* many "dads spent only eight minutes a day interacting with their children in such intense one-on-one activities as reading and personal conversation. The moms didn't do much better; they devoted only eleven minutes a day to activities with their children."

Reflections:

Freud said there are two requisites for human happiness: work and love. When work becomes all consuming and we shut ourselves off from the loving support of our families, something inside us dies. When we're too busy to attend a recital, too tired to put up a basketball hoop, too distracted to help with homework, something is wrong at the very core of our being. We've lost sight of why we're working and for whom. In the final analysis, our most important job is that of loving spouse and parent.

Today I'm going to take the whole family out to a restaurant where we can all talk.

MARCH 22

"If you become that successful manager, you will face the truth of the required personal sacrifice every day at 5 P.M."
—Harold Geneen

During his reign at ITT, Harold Geneen introduced "management by meeting" with many grueling sessions lasting far into the night. At the end of one such meeting, the members adjourned to a nearby restaurant to continue their discussions at 2:00 a.m. At that point, Geneen asked, "What special quality are we looking for in ITT executives which will differentiate them from other company executives?" "Insomnia," volunteered one executive.

Reflections:

Harold Geneen, and people like him, are blessed with extraordinary energy, which enables them to work tirelessly at their jobs. Work is a major theme of their life, a driving passion, demanding total commitment by these executives and all who surround them. Geneen inspired awe and dedication among the staff who worked closely with him. Those who couldn't or didn't want to keep up were left behind. But when the price of success includes the sacrifice of your personal life, it's time to redefine what you mean by success.

To better manage my time, I'll have my secretary schedule my appointments.

*"Dear God, I pray for patience. And, I
want it right now!"*

—Oren Arnold

We workaholics must be close "kin" to the man
in the Talmudic tale who rushed past Rabbi Ben
Meir of Berchidev. "My friend," the rabbi called after him, "where are you off to in such a great hurry?" "I cannot stop to talk," the man called back,
"I'm running after my livelihood." "And how do
you know," answered the rabbi, "that your livelihood is running on before you so that you have to
rush after it? Perhaps it's behind you, and all you
have to do is stand still."

Reflections:

We all need to stop at times to reflect on where
we have been and where we are going. This is especially true of the workaholic, whose breakneck
pursuit of success often leads nowhere. If your busy
schedule does not allow you enough time to pray-
erfully reflect on your business decisions, consider
the words of Martin Luther: "I have so much business," he said, "I cannot get on without spending
three hours a day in prayer."

*Instead of pursuing serenity, I must let it overtake
me.*

> *"There is an appointed time for every-*
> *thing and a time for every affair under*
> *the heavens."*
>
> —Ecclesiastes 3:1

Most workaholics are familiar with time man-agement principles, but we tend to interpret them as getting more done in less time. "Getting things done" places the emphasis on doing things right rather than on doing the right things. True time management requires us to manage our decisions and set realistic goals before we set our schedule. Until then, we'll remain in the same time bind that Henry Kissinger found himself in as Secretary of State. "There cannot be a crisis next week," he said. "My schedule is already full."

Reflections:

Are you working longer hours, handling one crisis after another? Do you feel unappreciated at work? Are you chronically tired, irritable, and de-pressed? If so, you could be among the 60 percent of all managers who have experienced burnout, ac-cording to a study by the American Management So-ciety. The underlying cause of burnout, say psychologists, is the repeated failure to achieve "un-realistic goals." If you're feeling burned out, or crisp around the edges, it could be time to reexamine your priorities.

I'm going to do the right things, and do them right.

"'Late' is a four-letter word."
          —Sign in a workaholic's office

The speed required to exploit short-term competitive advantages, the need to satisfy market demand and the delays in any project create tremendous time pressures on you as a manager. The greater the pressure to perform, the greater the likelihood of compromise during the final stages of a program. The temptation you face in such situations is to rush to finish the work, skipping important steps, just to get the project done.

Reflections:

Life isn't a hundred-yard dash. It's more like a steeplechase with obstacles and hurdles laid out on an oval track. The real hazard in a steeplechase isn't the hurdles you can see; it's the extra ten strides you have to run each lap when someone bumps you into the next lane over. Instead of always jostling for position, lay back, hug the inside track, and save your kick for the end. The race is won, or lost, in the last fifty yards.

Like anyone who has ever won a foot race, I must take one step at a time.

"It's a poor sort of memory that only works backwards."

—Lewis Carroll

Looking backward, our imaginations are capable of prodigious feats; looking forward is another matter. The truth is, most of us are more at home in the past. In fact, we are immersed in the past at this very moment; the clothes we wear, the chair we sit on, the room we occupy in the house where we live, are all part of our living past. That is one reason why old habits, like workaholism, are so hard to change: they are part of the furniture of our mind.

Reflections:

The future, however, is a strange and foreign place that can only be reached by changing. The question is, what kind of changes are we prepared to make? They need not be great ones; they can be as simple as taking a lunch-hour walk or reading a book at night. Pick one goal for each day, and hold that image in your mind until you've accomplished it. See yourself changing and succeeding. As John Henry Newman said, "The essence of life is change and the essence of perfection is to change often."

I began by forming work habits; now my work habits form me.

MARCH 27

"We often tend to be marching backwards to the future."
—Paul Valery

Astronomers studying a quasar 13,000 billion light years away have observed that its light waves are actually bent by the gravitational field of an intervening galaxy. Incredibly, the bent rays act as light particles when measured by one device, and as light waves when measured by another device. We are measuring something that happened millions of years ago and somehow changing it here and now.

Reflections:

If we can change the course of light waves that occurred in the dim and distant past, how much easier must it be to change the course of brain waves called *memories* that illuminate our universe within. To change our attitudes and feelings about work, we must choose a different measuring device just as the astronomers did. Instead of measuring success by wealth, power, or prestige, we need to look at self-actualization and altruism. Then our thinking will be light years ahead.

My attitude toward work is becoming better every day.

*"Better one word in time than two after-
wards."*

—Welsh proverb

In the course of your career, you will spend
three full years on the telephone, often "on hold."
Yet the phone can be one of your most productive
business tools, and learning to use it properly can
increase your effectiveness while reducing your
stress. Using the phone may seem as natural as talking, but it is more complex—just look at all the buttons on your phone, if you have any doubts. Chances
are, like many executives, you've never learned to
use all those whistles and bells!

Reflections:

The new telecommunications systems offer a
wide range of time-saving features such as "confer-
ence call," "call waiting," "queuing," "messaging,"
and "voice mail." If you're not using the full capa-
bilities of your system, you're wasting time in telephone tag. Of course, you don't need all those
buttons to be more efficient on the phone. Simple
things like preparing beforehand can save time. So,
too, can having your secretary include return numbers on every phone memo. Why not start today to
use the phone more efficiently?

*I have to learn how to "ring" the most out of my
phone.*

MARCH 29

"The computer is a moron."
—Peter Drucker

Business is a contact sport—if you're out of contact, you're out of business. With today's laptop portable computers, you can access every file in your desk, day or night, at home or on the road. However, the computer's convex screen can also act like a lens, distorting your thinking, pricking your anxieties with each new blip that says, "RUN ... RUN ... RUN." In synchronization with the computer, you start to make decisions faster and faster, as if the quality of your ideas could be expressed in baud rates.

Reflections:
You know it's time to hit the "home" cursor when you catch yourself acting as if "It's not what you know that counts. It's what you think of in time." Quality decisions require time in which to mull over the facts, consult with others, and consider alternatives. It's not enough to think it up; you have to think it through. Sometimes, when you're pressed for an answer, the best response is "I don't know—let me think about it."

If I'm only as good as my next idea, I'd better make it good.

*"What people don't understand is that
there really are more than twenty-four
hours in a day."*

—T. Boone Pickens

T. Boone Pickens, the corporate raider, is a former college athlete. To him, business is a game of
basketball, where you fast break every chance you
get and full court press on defense. There are no
time-outs for breathers; no half-time breaks; it's run-
and-gun all the way, with one eye on the shot clock.
He routinely works twelve-hour days and expects
his staff to do the same. Pickens not only works
hard, he also plays hard at tennis, racquetball, and
golf. He also works out daily in the physical fitness
center in his corporate headquarters.

Reflections:

It's a physiological fact that exercise increases
our metabolic rate, and, as our own internal clock
speeds up, we feel as if time had slowed down. So
it could well be that T. Boone Pickens does feel like
there are more than twenty-four hours in his day.
How much exercise do you get daily?

*I'm going to get at least twenty minutes of aerobic
exercise a day.*

MARCH 31

"Those who speak most of progress measure it by quantity and not by quality."
—George Santyana

The glossy brochures that accompany personal computers encourage you to run several routines at once—edit one document, mail-merge a second, and print a third, simultaneously. Technology has pushed the boundaries of time beyond the limits of human comprehension and has forced us to operate outside our comfort zone. We work fifty to sixty hours a week, and still we are overwhelmed by the onslaught of E-mail, voice mail, trade journals, technical reports, and new product bulletins that undermine our most fundamental assumptions about business.

Reflections:

There is an upper limit to our physical ability to absorb the information generated by change. Most of us still read at a rate of 350–400 words a minute. We can only hear 275–300 words a minute, speak 120–140 words a minute, and write 45–60 words a minutes. Our ability to express information in human terms has not changed in millennia. As we move to a high-tech, information-intensive society, the rate of change threatens to overwhelm us. One way to buffer yourself against the onslaught is by focusing on one area and becoming a specialist.

I'm going to develop an area of expertise.

APRIL

Ambition

We have a strong need for recognition and tangible evidence that our lives amount to something. Often our ambitions become grandiose and unrealistic, but in our desire to appear successful, we pay any price—including the sacrifice of our true feelings. We have to accept the fact that we are not perfect, and we need to make an honest appraisal of our strengths, weaknesses, and potential.

APRIL 1

"All sins have their origin in a sense of inferiority, otherwise called ambition."
—Cesare Pavese

When the alumni magazine arrives at your house, what's the first thing you read? Chances are, you turn to the page listing career changes, and run your finger down the dates until you find the year you graduated. Then you read about all the honors, awards, and titles that have been heaped on people whose grade-point average was *at least* one-half point lower than yours; and you go into a deep blue funk wondering why it seems like every other person has won a Nobel Prize, been elected state senator, or in some other way passed you by in the race for success. Must we always compete—even with people we haven't seen in years?

Reflections:

There's only one person you can beat every time, and that's yourself. So long as your self-worth is based on achievement rather than on self-actualization, you are going to lose out to the gold-plated plastic image of yourself standing on a trophy case in a corner of your mind. True satisfaction is derived, not from winning, but from the exploration and development of whatever talents you've been given.

My ambition is to make the most of my talents.

APRIL 2

"The urgent problems are seldom the important ones."

—Former President
Dwight D. Eisenhower

Many executives view a long project list as a sign of ambition. But a lengthy project list can also be a sign of poor delegation, unfocused effort, and a lack of planning. The fact that you're handling many projects suggests that you are efficient, but not necessarily effective. The art of project management lies in identifying the 20 percent of your projects that produce 80 percent of the results so you can concentrate on them. Once you establish your priorities, guard them jealously. The truly important tasks seldom have to be done immediately, and as a result they can be easily delayed.

Reflections:

In reviewing your project list, rank each task by priority; then arrange them in three columns with most important projects in the left-hand column, the next most important in the middle, and the least important tasks on the right. Ask yourself whether any of them can be delegated or eliminated. Then concentrate on the most important ones. When they are completed, move on.

My ambition is to have a shorter project list in the afternoon than in the morning.

APRIL 3

"By working faithfully eight hours a day,
you may eventually get to be a boss and
work twelve hours a day."
—Robert Frost

From grade school on, we are entrained in the U.S. work ethic so that we never really question the assumptions on which our ambition is based. We're told, "The more you sweat, the more you get"; "No pain, no gain"; and "The harder you work, the luckier you get." Each of these statements is generally true, but they also imply that you can never work hard enough and that work is an end unto itself.

Reflections:

Work is at the very core of human existence, but when it is characterized by compulsive, unrelenting effort, it becomes workaholism. If you find yourself saying, "I have to work tonight," ask yourself, "Why?" The average executive works less than twenty hours a week to provide food, clothing, and shelter for his or her family. The rest of the time is spent working to acquire labor-saving devices and other creature comforts. Doesn't make much sense, does it?

I'll count myself a success when I stop counting all my successes.

*"We need the courage to start and con-
tinue what we should do, and courage to
stop what we shouldn't do."*
—Richard L. Evans

Imagine for a moment that you have been invited to deliver the commencement address to the
graduating class of your alma mater five years from
now. In introducing you to the assembly, the dean
of the college describes the high points of your career, with special emphasis on the last few years.
Since we're describing future events, give your
imagination free rein, and envision yourself achieving the type of goals you would set for yourself if
you knew you couldn't fail.

Reflections:
What would those goals be? And, how would
you describe for those students the steps you took
to achieve your ambition? They're young and
impressionable, as you once were, and in their ide-
alism they believe anything is possible. All they
need is a goal and a dream. When you stop to think
about it, the same is true of us all. We don't close
our minds when we close our books. We don't stop
dreaming and imagining. The truth is, we start our
careers over every single day. Isn't it time you started acting out your dreams for the next five years?

Every step toward my goal is also a leap of faith.

"If you don't have a destination, you'll never get there."

—Harvey Mackay

Harvey Mackay, the irrepressible supersalesman who built a multimillion-dollar company, kept on the inside of his hatband the business card of his largest sales prospect. Before making his daily rounds, he looked at that card, imagined himself succeeding, and eventually turned that prospect into a customer. Of course, we all have goals for each new day. But the type of goals that truly inspire us are the larger, longer-range ones that require exceptional effort and prayer.

Reflections:

In the Old Testament, the Jews were led through the desert by a pillar of fire at night and a cloud by day. It was their ever-present goal. We all need goals in life; without them, our work becomes boring, mindless activity. Are your goals big enough to let God in? Have you written them out in detail along with due dates? Have you shared your goals with at least one person, so that you are committed to them? Are you taking steps to achieve them? Have you turned to prayer for guidance?—often the biggest strides are made while on our knees.

Today, I'm going to set a goal that is impossible without God.

"Anything worth doing is worth overdoing."

—Motto of a workaholic

In the early days of Apple Computer, a common sight on the company's campus was employees in T-shirts silk-screened with the words "Working fifty hours a week and loving it." Those words would be crossed out and replaced with "Working seventy hours a week and loving it." And, that saying would be replaced by "Working ninety hours a week and loving it." The employees' faces were lined with sleeplessness, but their eyes sparkled with ambition. What accounted for their ability to work at a harried pace? And, can such a pace be maintained without burning out?

Reflections:

These were all young, energetic people who believed their "mission" was to bring computer power to humanity. They were led by Steven Jobs, a charismatic visionary who inspired and challenged them to do something "Insanely great!" But it's worth noting that Jobs himself took on too much, and when the Macintosh office failed to materialize, he lost his position. Are you taking on more than you can handle? Are your goals ambitious, or are they insanely great?

My first job is to set realistic goals.

"One man with courage makes a majority."

—Andrew Jackson

The undoing of many a workaholic has not been a lack of ambition; it's been a lack of courage. We always seem to have the ambition to take on one more problem, one more assignment when what is really called for is the courage to say no. We need to decide which battles are worth fighting, or we will discover what the Greek commander Pyrrhus meant when he said "One more such victory and we are done for."

Reflections:

It's true in battle and it's true in business: the first test of your ambition is knowing when to take a stand. To achieve victory in battle, you must concentrate your forces in overwhelming mass and in so doing take a risk. To achieve success in business, you must focus your resources on the greatest opportunities. You can't afford to pursue several conflicting objectives simultaneously, waiting to see what happens, letting necessity do the work of courage. You must decide.

I need a little less ambition and a little more gumption.

"The path of least resistance is a bog."
—Bob Larrañaga

Whether it's a sales contract, a compensation package, a mortgage, or an equipment lease, most of us are impatient with the whole process of bargaining. The uncertainty surrounding negotiations thwarts our need for control. In our eagerness to get to yes, we may take the path of least resistance and make one concession after another. Too late, we discover the power of a positive no—we're bogged down in an unworkable agreement.

Reflections:

Chances are, you're accustomed to accepting most challenges that cross your desk. In true workaholic fashion, you may seldom say no. To say so would be to draw the line and state your limits. But you're not willing to concede any limits, not without trying. However, when it comes to negotiations, you can't afford to be so eager. If you're not prepared to say no, bring a negotiator who is; otherwise you may squander your money, time, and talent on projects that aren't worth the commitment in resources. Saying no may be the most ambitious statement you can make today.

No one will place more value on my services than I do.

APRIL 9

"There is no job so simple that it cannot be done wrong."

—Anonymous

The Greek god Proteus was the original workaholic. He played so many roles (lion, dragon, and roaring fire) that he seldom used his own unique gift of prophecy. Many workaholics suffer the same fate—we do not achieve our ambition because we dissipate our energy and talent jumping from one job to the next. In our pell-mell pursuit of success, we're never in one position long enough to master it. Eventually, our overworked résumés make it difficult for us to find a job.

Reflections:

Does your résumé say you want "an executive position in a growing company where I can make a meaningful contribution." Recruiters say such a vague ambition indicates a person in search of an identity. They may be right—maintaining a strong self-image *is* difficult. We all play many roles in our daily lives, and we are never fully conscious of who we are because our self-images are blurred around the edges by wishful thinking. The key to a strong self-image is identifying our strengths and focusing on them. What's the one task you are best at?

I'm going to emphasize my strengths, not my weaknesses.

APRIL 10

"What's not worth doing is not worth doing well."

—Don Hebb

Many workaholics have something in common with the president of a firm whose ambitious expansion plans backfired and drained his company of working capital. In a meeting with the firm's bankers, the entrepreneur remained confident of his strategy; not so the skeptical bankers. After reviewing the results of the diversifications, the lending officer put it this way, "This company can be anything you want. It just can't be everything you want." The entrepreneur sold the money-losing subsidiaries and returned to profitability.

Reflections:

Which of us hasn't engaged in grandiose thinking at some time? We set unrealistic goals and strive to achieve them at all cost. We are Don Quixote in a three-piece suit, tilting after windmills in search of the Holy Grail. We dream impossible dreams and delight in projecting into the future where we seem to have complete control (at least for the present) over the outcome of our decisions. Our five-year plans are always optimistic. But until we accept the fact that we can't achieve all our ambitions, we are not prepared to pay the true price of success.

My first goal must be to realistically assess my abilities.

> *"To accomplish big things, I am con-*
> *vinced, you must first dream big*
> *dreams."*
>
> —Conrad Hilton

Conrad Hilton was a down-and-out Texan exist-
ing on a loan from a bellboy, his laundry in hock,
and a gun-toting constable posting court judgments
against him. But when he saw his first photograph
of New York's famous Waldorf Astoria Hotel and
read about its luxurious appointments, an ambition
took shape. He scrawled across the clipping, "The
greatest of them all," and later explained, "As soon
as I had won back a desk of my own, I slipped the
dog-eared clipping under the glass top. From then
on, it was always in front of me." Fifteen years later,
"The greatest hotel of them all" was a Hilton Hotel.

Reflections:

Conrad Hilton attributed his success to prayer,
work, and a dream. What is remarkable about his
story is the clarity of that dream and the way in
which it focused all his energies. As he said, "It was
always in front of me." By contrast, we sometimes
squander our prodigious energies on unfocused activities and poorly thought-out goals. If you can't
write your number one business goal on the back of
your calling card, you don't need a bigger card—you
need a more focused goal.

I need to focus my energy on a truly meaningful
goal.

APRIL 12

"Success has made failures of many men."

—Cindy Adams

Richard Hernnstein and James Mazur of Harvard University have conducted experiments showing that people are shortsighted in setting goals. We attach undue importance to short-term results and underestimate long-term consequences of our actions. We try to maximize our position in every case, and fail to see when the overall results would be better if we reduced returns in one sector (say, by making one product a loss leader). Most people, concluded the professors, treat every problem as a separate case instead of developing an overarching strategy.

Reflections:

We must be willing to let go of some opportunities in order to grasp other, bigger opportunities. It's an easy concept to understand, but a difficult one for ambitious workaholics to live by. We want to win every time, regardless of the ultimate cost. Our motto seems to be, "Nothing succeeds like excess." Consider today's project list, and ask yourself if there is one project you can eliminate so you can focus your energies.

A short project list is a sign that my energies are focused.

APRIL 13

"Never confuse motion with action."
—Ernest Hemingway

Some years ago, *Harvard Business Review* compared the career earnings of executives who had changed jobs several times with those of executives who had been loyal to one firm for the same period. Surprisingly, the loyal executives' earnings were comparable to those of the job hoppers who had paid a much higher personal price and had assumed larger risks to achieve their ambitions. This story should serve as a cautionary tale for workaholics. Our driving ambition makes us vulnerable to the blandishments of executive recruiters who promise to let you "run your own shop" at another company.

Reflections:

The higher you climb on the ladder of success, the further apart the rungs might appear. You have to grow into each new job before you can take the next step up. If your upward progress is slowed, you may be tempted to change jobs. But many of your hard-earned skills may not be transferable, and what appears to be a step up may actually be a weak rung. Take your time in considering any job offers. Make sure the ladder you are climbing is leaning against the right building.

I need the patience to take one step at a time.

"We work to become, not to acquire."
—Elbert Hubbard

Our self-worth and identity are often equated with our position in the corporate hierarchy. But with each move up, the competition increases, and the footing becomes more precarious. Of every 1,000 senior executives, 453 will not be in the same position a year from now. Some of your peers may have received their last promotion, and others may already have had their exit interviews. If your grip on the ladder is a bit shaky, too, you may be plagued by doubts and fears. At times like this, a few moments of quiet reflection can help you regain your balance.

Reflections:

Take a look at your business card. Chances are, your job title contains no more than two or three words. All your hard work, all those years of relentless effort, can be summed up in two or three words. It's a funny thing about job titles—you spend the better part of your life working to earn them, but when it comes time to memorialize you, they don't chisel "Vice President" on your tombstone. They chisel "Devoted Spouse," or "Loving Spouse." If you're doing well at those two jobs, you're a success, no matter what rung you're standing on.

I'm going to work harder at being a family member.

APRIL 15

"There is no failure except in no longer trying."

—Elbert Hubbard

According to Robert Hecht (co-chairman of Lee Hecht Harrison, a large out-placement firm), the odds of losing your current job are one in three, and the higher you go in the organization, the greater the odds become. To a workaholic, whose whole life centers around the job, unemployment can be a devastating experience. At times like this, when the path to the top is obscured, keep in mind that faith can move mountains.

Reflections:

One-time mountain climber Tim Hansel could have been speaking for any workaholic on the downward slope of his career when he said, "Faith isn't faith until it's all you're holding on to." Hansel literally fell off a mountain, miraculously survived, and turned his shattered hopes and dreams into a successful career. Anyone who has gone mountain climbing or has tried to scale the pinnacle of success, knows that the most difficult path is straight up. If you find yourself stumbling, change the angle of your ascent, but keep on moving in the right direction.

The size of my steps isn't as important as the direction I take.

"It's great to be great, but it's greater to be human."

—Will Rogers

The down-sizing of U.S. industry has significantly increased the work load of the remaining executives, according to a study by Opinion Research. The survey of three thousand managers showed that 30 percent are experiencing increased work pressures. The situation in one company was caricatured by a sign posted on a vending machine: "In this department everyone is expected to do the work of two men—Laurel and Hardy."

Reflections:

In our all-consuming ambition, we workaholics sometimes accept a punishing work load. In our minds, saying no to an assignment would be tantamount to failing without trying. Since we tend to think in terms of all or nothing, saying no would mean complete defeat. Given this extreme view, our only recourse is to say yes and try to make a superhuman effort. When we fail, as we inevitably must, the cycle repeats itself until, exhausted, we are forced to admit our limitations.

My inability to say no could be a sign of false pride.

APRIL 17

*"You know you're successful when you
no longer do anything you're good at."*
—Deborah Gellbach

Over 50 percent of the labor force works for organizations that employ over a hundred people, and 33 percent work for organizations of more than five hundred people. The higher up you go in these bureaucracies, the further removed you become from the front-line, day-to-day activities. The work becomes more abstract, the meetings run longer, and the lead times stretch out interminably. For a hands-on, action-oriented workaholic, a corner office job can be deadly dull.

Reflections:

In planning your career, you'll want to look for a job that offers a challenge, variety, and a certain amount of autonomy. The pitfall many workaholics fall into is accepting a job that emphasizes their weaknesses instead of their strengths. We're drawn to outward signs of success, positions of authority, and impressive-sounding titles. But the prestige of the position we covet can blind us to the fact that we don't enjoy being administrators or bureaucrats. We're shirt-sleeves executives, and our strength lies in implementation, not administration.

I'm at my best when the job calls for resourcefulness.

APRIL 18

"One of the symptoms of an approaching nervous breakdown is the belief that one's work is terribly important."
—Bertrand Russell

How often have you pushed yourself past the point of exhaustion, relying on willpower and stimulants to charge ahead? In such an embattled state, your body may be ready to surrender to sleep, but your mind keeps sniping at the problems that have dogged your steps, like a shadow, for twelve hours. You toss and turn in your pillow bunker, waiting for the dawn and the sound of the alarm, when you can leap from your foxhole and attack the problem again.

Reflections:

When your sleep habits are disrupted, your thought patterns become confused, paranoid, and suspicious. You may develop a negative, defeatist attitude in the face of problems that seem overwhelming. The less sleep you get, the worse the problems appear and the more dependent you become on depressants and stimulants. To restore your sanity, flush the pills down the drain and spend half an hour before bedtime with an inspirational book. Remember, sleep is not the enemy.

I'm going to get the rest I need to handle my work load.

*"If you don't get the better of yourself,
someone else will."*

—Anonymous

"I don't get ulcers, I give them," is the hollow
boast of many a workaholic. Any sign of illness is
seen by workaholics as failure. We may come to the
office with a head cold, fever, and strep throat. We
may suffer bouts of anxiety-induced diarrhea, migraine headaches, back spasms, and insomnia. And,
bravado aside, we may also suffer from ulcers. But
we refuse to submit to our infirmities, until the in-
cline on the treadmill is so steep that we topple
backward into a hospital bed.

Reflections:

The link between workaholism and health is
not straightforward. Each of us has a different capacity for handling job pressures. The symptoms of
burnout vary from individual to individual and may
occur sporadically. As a result, it is easy to attribute
our ailments to "something that's going around." In
fact, one study showed that only 12 out of 450 business owners correctly identified their symptoms as
related to stress. If you're working twelve or more
hours a day, you can safely assume you are over-
stressed.

*I'm going to get off the treadmill and go for a lei-
surely walk.*

"All work and no play makes Jack a dull boy—and Jill a wealthy widow."
—Evan Esar

When work becomes the driving passion of our lives, the goal is no longer success, but rather fatigue. We begin to pursue hard work and the fatigue it brings, as the only way to find surcease from our restless, driving ambition. No matter how well we're doing, our stock answer is "Things could be better"—that's all the excuse we need to continue working. Only when we're exhausted do we feel as though we've done enough. By then, we're too weak and tired to enjoy what real success we've earned.

Reflections:

All our long hours and hard work may not pay off in the end. Many workaholics are dead-ended in the middle of what began as promising careers because they're disruptive, competitive, and create morale problems. Those who manage to get closer to the top discover it is an empty success, because they long ago lost sight of why they work so hard. The few who reach the very pinnacle may learn that the descent is far faster than the ascent.

I'll pick a firm time at the end of each day for wrapping up business.

*"Destiny is not a matter of chance, it is
a matter of choice."*
—William Jennings Bryan

To hear them talk, if it weren't for bad luck some people would have no luck at all. Every problem is a catastrophe. They exaggerate the importance of bad news and convince themselves that things won't work out. Their negative attitude becomes a self-fulfilling prophecy and reinforces their pessimism. Their fatalistic thinking is revealed in such statements as "You can't fight city hall," "What's the use!" and "If anything can go wrong, it will." These comments are rationalizations of failure and mark the onset of burnout.

Reflections:

Burnout begins gradually, almost imperceptibly, as the result of unrealistic expectations. If you seem to be working harder and harder to accomplish less and less; if you are cynical, disenchanted with your job, and feel chronically tired, you could be burning out. The people most susceptible to burnout are the dynamic, goal-oriented, overachievers who have very high personal standards. Accustomed to working hard to achieve success, they fail to recognize that some situations are thankless and that no amount of effort can succeed.

I'm going to set a realistic goal and plan a reward ceremony for when I achieve it.

APRIL 22

"Too much is never enough."
—Mark Twain

Most workaholics experience initial success in their companies, their hard work rewarded by more hard work until they reach the level of mental, physical, and psychological exhaustion called *burnout.* Paradoxically, the harder they continue to work, the less productive they become and the more apparent their deficiencies are to management. Left to their own devices, they try to work their way through their problems, convinced that if they just work a little harder, a little longer, they can get on top of the work load.

Reflections:

Workaholism differs from most other types of compulsive behavior (such as gambling and drinking) in that we can't avoid it—we have to work! What's more, in our culture, workaholism is viewed as a virtue, and anyone unwilling to give his or her all to the company is considered a "shirkaholic." It's best not to say anything about your recovery program at work. Just quietly resolve to change for the better one day at a time. Why not start by eliminating the caffeine and sweet snacks that fuel your workaholism and contribute to your "Twinkies tantrums?"

I'm going to cut back on coffee and sweets.

"To do great work a man must be very idle as well as very industrious."
—Samuel Butler

The stereotype image of a burned-out executive is that of someone who never makes it to the top, whose reach exceeds his or her grasp, and whose ambition gives way to anger at the system. Perhaps that is true in many cases, but it is also true that some burnout cases have actually achieved their ambition—only to realize, too late, that it wasn't worth the price they paid. The root cause of burnout is an unrealistic, grandiose goal that by its very nature can never be fulfilling, no matter how successful you become.

Reflections:

If you are prepared to sacrifice intimate relationships, outside interests, and any strong personal feelings in pursuit of a career goal, you'd better ready yourself for a disappointment. The good life portrayed in the liquor, auto, and cosmetic ads is a chimera because it creates the illusion that happiness is the privilege of the rich, powerful, and famous. In reality, the loftiest ambition you can aspire to is to be at peace with yourself.

My ambition today is to find a few peaceful moments to myself.

APRIL 24

*"Is not life a hundred times too short for
us to bore ourselves?"*
—Friedrich Nietzsche

The opposite of work is not play. Work carried
to the opposite extreme is boredom—dull, unimaginative, mindless routine. Work can become boring
when we fail to develop vivid goals. Goals inspire
and motivate us to make the most of every opportunity life presents to us. They enable us to see more
in the situation than is actually there. In effect, goals
transform a job into a career. They energize us.

Reflections:

When was the last time you updated your career
goals? Have you written them out in vivid detail,
bringing into play all the senses? Can you see yourself succeeding? Does your image of success extend
beyond your career to include your family, friends,
and other outside interests? Create a vibrant image
in your mind, written out in detail, and list the steps
necessary to reach your goal. Then backtrack in your
mind to where you are today. Now that you know
the way, start taking the first steps to your goal.

*If the excitement has gone out of my present job, it's
time to reexamine my career goals.*

"There is no achievement without goals."

—Robert J. McKain

In a sense, each of us is like the battery that powers the calculator we use to put numbers to our dreams. The battery's zinc outer cylinder is analogous to our body, the catalyst inside is our mind, and the carbon core down the center is our spirit. The three are inert until some empowering goal unites body, mind, and spirit, the way a wire connects the electrodes in a battery. Suddenly, the current flows, and we're capable of doing great things. We're energized by our goals. But just as in a battery, our power can run down if the wire isn't removed. We need time to recharge ourselves.

Reflections:

Chances are, you chose your line of work because it energized you. You couldn't wait to get to work in the morning. Your mind ran ahead of you, thinking up new challenges, new ideas to be explored. That's the way it should be. But eventually your body catches up with your mind, and when it does you have to recognize that you're tired and you've earned your rest. Learn to unhook from the cares of your job by finding outside interests that bring you in contact with people who are interested in you as a person, rather than in you, the worker.

Instead of always focusing on ends, I need to focus on friends.

"Life is what happens to us while we are making other plans."
—Thomas LaMance

Early in his career, conglomerator Norton Simon bought an old orange juice plant in California with the idea of tearing it down and selling the scrap metal. But before he could do so, New York City scrapped the Second Avenue El, which depressed prices for all scrap metal. Simon's response was to go into the orange juice business for real, a move that eventually led to acquisition of a tomato-processing plant and other food companies, which together formed a multibillion-dollar corporate giant. Life had handed Norton Simon a lemon, and he turned it into orange juice.

Reflections:

The resilience that distinguishes so many successful people comes naturally to workaholics. Faced with a problem, you will no doubt do everything in your power to solve it. But sometimes the best solution lies not in fighting the problem, but in accepting it as an opportunity and working smarter to make the most of it the way Norton Simon did. Is there a problem on your desk now that needs rethinking?

The solution to my problems is not to work harder, but smarter.

"I am the master of my fate; I am the captain of my soul."
—William E. Henley

One distinguishing characteristic of workaholics is our passion for achievement. The energy and drive with which we tackle obstacles, overcome problems, and rebound from setbacks, accounts for a large measure of our success. Of all the jobs we take on, none requires more persistence and resilience than overcoming our own workaholism. There may be relapses, but we can't become discouraged, give in, and say, "What's the use?" We have to fight to preserve our private life with all the tenacity we normally reserve for business.

Reflections:

Self-awareness is simply not enough to affect a change in your work habits. You have to change your attitude toward work because it is going to take a strong emotional commitment to a new and richer lifestyle to see you through the difficult times when work seems all consuming. Each small change in behavior reinforces your new attitude and stimulates within your imagination a vivid picture of what life can be like when work and leisure are in balance.

I'm up to the job of learning how to relax.

"Most people give up just when they're
about to achieve success"
—H. Ross Perot

In his fifth year with IBM, Ross Perot sold his year's quota in the first three weeks; but to his chagrin his reward was a desk job. Then he read in Thoreau, "The mass of men lead lives of quiet desperation" and decided to form Electronic Data Systems with $1,000 of savings. In twenty two years, he built EDS into a 45,000-employee firm, which General Motors bought for $991 million. Yet the center of Perot's life remained his family. "If I could do one thing," he told a reporter, "I would try to construct a strong family unit for every family (in the United States) on the basis of love, understanding, and encouragement."

Reflections:

Often the real casualties of our workaholic ambitions are our families. Work becomes so demanding that spouses and children must fend for themselves. The situation was epitomized by an incident involving a workaholic whose wife expected a visit from her mother. When she told their daughter they'd soon have a visitor they hadn't seen in a long, long time, the child squealed in delight, "Daddy!" How ambitious are your plans for your family? How many hours a week do you spend with them?

I'm going to plan a family outing for this weekend.

"People with goals succeed because they know where they're going."
—Earl Nightingale

The Jews of the Old Testament knew their goal was the Promised Land. But they wandered aimlessly through the desert for forty years on a journey that should have taken eleven days. They complicated their lives every time they wandered from the path of simplicity laid out for them in the New Covenant. How often do you think through your goals in life and decide the steps you'll take to achieve them?

Reflections:

"Simplicity" is an overarching strategy for achieving life's goals. It forces you to rank goals and to accept the fact that every time you add something to your life, you have to let go of something else. If your long-range goals and short-range goals are inconsistent, if you have too many goals, or if you have conflicting goals, you'll complicate your life. Simplicity forces you to decide what's important in life, what price you'd pay for it, and the steps you must take to achieve it.

To achieve success, I must embrace simplicity.

APRIL 30

"Leisure comes to all when day's work is over."

—Anonymous

It's possible to become addicted to work. The hormones secreted when you're competing at the office create a natural high that makes it difficult to unwind on weekends. Compared to work, everything else seems boring, so you may even compete at play. Do you engage in sports that are highly demanding, competitive, and exhausting? Do you keep score, clock yourself, weigh in, and weigh out? Instead of relaxing on your days off, are you competing at the same level of intensity that you bring to work? Does your body get a chance to rest and recuperate? Does your ambition know no bounds?

Reflections:

You wouldn't be a workaholic without the extraordinary amount of nervous energy that fuels your relentless drive to win at all costs. The urge to compete, however, can blind you to physical and mental fatigue. You may even come to think of exhaustion as a sign of weakness or a lack of commitment. To regain your perspective, you need to take time off each weekend to enjoy yourself in noncompetitive activities.

This weekend, I'm going to rest up with a good book.

MAY

Problem Solving

When faced with a problem, we may overreact because we feel threatened by a loss of control. The ambiguity and complexity of the situation frustrates us, and in our perplexed state we may oversimplify things or jump to the wrong conclusion. We have to change our way of thinking and be willing to admit to others when we are wrong.

MAY 1

*"Life is not a problem to be solved, but
a reality to be experienced."*
—Søren Kierkegaard

A workaholic is someone who has a problem for
every solution. We approach life as though it were a
string of problems, a series of knots to be untied,
one leading to another in never-ending succession. I
"must" do this; I "should" do that; the sheer number of problems becomes a problem in itself. The
reality is we're the ones that tied the knots in the
first place. We're the ones who created the problems
by trying so hard to control events that we simply
tied ourselves in knots.

Reflections:
Learning to laugh at our problems is tonic for
the body and soul. In fact, Norman Cousins, former
publisher of the *Saturday Review*, recovered from a
life-threatening illness by watching comedy movies.
Once you start laughing at the antics of comedians,
it's easier to laugh your own troubles away and experience the true joy of living. Why not rent a comedy video or buy a comedy audio cassette for your
car radio?

Grant me the humility to laugh at my problems.

MAY 2

*"The mark of a true M.B.A. is that he is
often wrong, but seldom in doubt."*
—Robert Buzzell

We tend to think of management errors as isolated events, or specific decisions of a strategic nature. Actually, most errors do not involve a conscious decision of any kind. A crucial moment passes unnoticed, and a decision is not made; or the consequences of our decisions unfold so slowly that we can't tell precisely where we went wrong. Everything blurs together in a scenario that leaves us confident that we did all that we could and that events were beyond our control.

Reflections:

Legendary venture capitalist Arthur Rock once said, "Strategy is easy, but tactics are hard." Success in business comes down to the way we handle the thousands of small, tactical decisions made every day. There are so many decisions that we make many of them reflexively, without thinking, relying on pat solutions that worked in the past. If we're workaholics, we confuse efficiency with effectiveness and don't take enough time to reflect on our situation. If you find yourself dealing with a recurring problem, it's time to examine your tactics.

A recurring problem is a symptom of a larger, underlying one.

MAY 3

"Think like a man of action, act like a man of thought."
—Henri Bergson

The way you cope with the surprising twists and turns of life is based on your preferred problem-solving strategy. As a workaholic, your bias for decisive, impulsive action leads to a trial-and-error, freewheeling approach to problems. Implicit in this strategy is the willingness to accept the first solution that satisfies the minimum acceptable conditions—as opposed to waiting for the optimum solution. This strategy usually works with fairly simple, low-risk problems where fast action is advantageous and where a mistake won't be costly. But with complex problems a more reflective problem-solving approach is needed.

Reflections:

When confronted with problems today, check your tendency to react instantly. The test of managers is not what they can do, but what their staff can do without them. Work through the chain of command, and seek the opinions of others. Chances are you'll get a new insight into the problem, and, possibly, discover a solution that involves working smarter, not harder.

When faced with a problem, the most important action I can take is to stop and think.

MAY 4

"There is no expedient to which a man will not resort to avoid the real labor of thinking."

—Sir Joshua Reynolds

As workaholics, our basic modality is one of action, rather than thoughtful reflection. We may even jump to erroneous conclusions because they are more attractive than the truth. For example, we may want to believe false rumors about a competitor because it makes us feel superior. Or we may prefer an interpretation that is simpler and tidier than the truth, which is often complex and at times, confusing. In our rush to judgment, we may believe what's comfortable to believe; that is, we may look for confirmation rather than information, and discount anything that doesn't fit our preconceived notions.

Reflections:

In one of the Marx Brothers movies, Zeppo turns to Chico and says, "We gotta *think*," to which Chico replies, "Naw—we already tried that." Once you've made up your mind on a subject, how open are you to rethinking your position? One mark of a successful executive is the ability to reexamine a strategy in light of new evidence and accept the truth, even when it's painful.

Sometimes the best decision is not to act, but to pray.

*"For every problem there is a solution
which is simple, neat and wrong."*
— H. L. Mencken

We tend to recognize problems that fit our own style of thinking, and ignore those that don't. For example, you might notice information-intensive problems (such as a high rate of absenteeism) while another executive might focus on subjective problems (employee morale). Both of you might fail to notice the two facts are related. Problem recognition is crucial because most business mistakes are errors of omission rather than commission: we don't see the problem until it is too late.

Reflections:

Although each of us has a preferred mode of thinking about problems, successful managers adapt their thinking to the situation. This flexibility enables them to consider more ideas and arrive at better informed decisions. We workaholics attack a problem one way: head on, relying on facts and figures, seldom on intuition. Make a special effort to look at business problems more than one way, especially when dealing with subjective values.

At times, it takes more courage to change my convictions than to hold to them.

MAY 6

*"The mind is its own place and in itself
can make a heaven a hell and a hell of
heaven."*

—John Milton

The human mind is extremely complex. There
are over fifteen billion neurons in the cerebral cor-
tex, and each neuron has axons and dendrites so
that there are over a hundred billion "wires" that
can short-circuit in our brains. When a nerve impulse activates other neurons, the pulse at the syn-
apse is so low that there is a large uncertainty as to
its exact location at any point in time. The very
pulse itself may be unstable. In other words, brain
waves—like ocean waves—are never the same twice.

Reflections:

In an effort to make sense of these shifting, tossing brain wave patterns, the mind erects breakwaters
or channels of thought—preconceived notions, biases, prejudices. Gradually, we cease to see what we're
looking at and begin to see what we're looking for:
ideas that fit our own viewpoint. When that happens, our judgment becomes flawed. We develop
channel thinking and overlook promising ideas. The
challenge is not only to think up solutions, but to
think them through.

*Today I will resist the urge to rush to judgment and
will seek the opinions of others.*

*"Life is the art of making decisions in
the absence of sufficient information."*
—Oliver Wendell Holmes

A hopeless muddle is a problem that someone
didn't break down into smaller steps. If the steps
can be defined and arranged in sequential order, the
problem is essentially one of scheduling. Unfortunately, we workaholics are not very good at sequential thinking. In our impatience, we skip steps. We
close our eyes to the amount of time it takes to perform each step and rush headlong into a series of
bottlenecks. Then we exhort our staff to blast
through the work jam by working overtime!

Reflections:

Nothing clarifies a problem like a little black
ink. When faced with a scheduling problem, it helps
to visualize the crucial path to a solution by writing
out the essential steps in sequential order. Next to
each step, indicate the most optimistic, probable,
and pessimistic time to perform that operation. Base
your planning on the most probable time line and
allow time for minor deviations. Chances are, your
schedule will be fairly realistic.

*I'm going to be more realistic in estimating the num-
ber of steps in a project and the time needed to complete them.*

MAY 8

"Those who mistake their good luck for their merit are inevitably bound for disaster."

—J. Christopher Herald

Many workaholics enjoy success early in their careers and begin to believe they can do no wrong. As their knowledge grows, their confidence in their problem-solving ability increases. Confronting a complex problem, they're apt to overestimate their analytical skills and predictive abilities and take unnecessary risks. They believe they're "lucky" and that the harder they work, the luckier they get. That may be true in an entry-level management position, but the higher up they go the more complex the problems become and the greater the chances for a run of "bad luck."

Reflections:

In solving complex problems, your chances of error increase exponentially as the number of steps to the solution increase linearly. Although the chance of an error is slight at any one stage, the probability of success may be very low if there are many steps. Moreover, your assessment of risk may be clouded by your knowledge of the subject and recall of details. Wishful thinking can cause you to disregard vital information and plunge ahead, confident things will work out.

I have to think through the risks before I plunge ahead.

"In the beginner's mind, there are many possibilities, but in the experts there are few."

—Shunryu Surjuki

As you become more expert in your profession, you naturally develop a set of problem-solving strategies. A systematic approach is faster and more efficient than groping toward a solution. However, it also results in fewer breakthrough ideas. For example, as an expert you might think the solution to a problem is as simple as "1 and 1 equals 2." But is it? The solution is 2, if you're using a decimal system. But what if you're using a binary system? In that case, the answer is 102? The moment you decide on a systematic approach to problem solving, you reduce the number of ideas considered.

Reflections:

The point is simply this: as a workaholic, you may favor a fast, efficient system of problem solving and consider other approaches as groping in the dark. But mathematics and logic—the language of business—are themselves second-order information-processing systems. You must first decide which numbers to count and which facts to analyze. Even though everything adds up to your way of thinking, you may still be wrong. Keep an open mind.

The only solution that makes sense is the one that works.

"I know that nothing belongs to me but the thought which unimpeded from my soul will flow."
—Johann Wolfgang von Goethe

All we truly own and possess—all we control—are our thoughts. And yet we try so hard to control other people and things that in the process we lose control of our thoughts. Problems come to dominate our thinking and rob us of our peace of mind. We lose sight of the fact that nothing is a problem unless we say it is; that we are a product of the choices we make. We can decide what we'll think about and how we'll think.

Reflections:

The measure of an executive is the size of the problems he or she chooses to solve. During the course of the day, many problems will cross your desk and your mind; if you try to solve every one of them, you'll never solve the important ones. The mistake most workaholics make is to say to themselves, "I'm too busy to delegate" or "I can do it faster and better." In the short run, that may be true; but in the long run, the time invested in delegation multiplies your effectiveness. Before tackling another assignment, ask yourself, "whose problem is this?"

The biggest step in solving a problem may be stepping aside so someone else can handle it.

MAY 11

*"Man's mind stretched to a new idea
never goes back to its original shape."*
—Oliver Wendell Holmes

In our quest of understanding, we instinctively
categorize everything we encounter according to
some fixed patterns in our mind. We even create patterns where none exist; the mind simply fills in the
blanks; rather than recognizing that some inputs are
nothing more than background noise, we assign
them a meaning. Often the patterns of thought exist
only in our imaginations—and no one else's—because we sort reality according to the spreadsheet
in the backs of our minds.

Reflections:

All categories are arbitrary. And since categori-
zation is the organizing principle of thought, all
thoughts are arbitrary. No one has all the answers.
Has your thinking become rigid and inflexible? Are
you open to new ways of doing business, new technology, and differing points of view? Although ca-
tegorization is normal and natural, truly creative
people show an ability to categorize the same thing
many different ways. They're constantly changing
and stretching to accommodate new ideas.

*I have to listen to the ideas of others as if they were
my own.*

MAY 12

"A belief is not merely an idea the mind possesses; it is an idea that possesses the mind."

—Robert Bolton

During the reign of King Louis XI of France, an astrologer accurately foretold the death of a lady in the king's court. Thinking the astrologer had caused the woman's death, the king summoned him to the palace where he planned to have the astrologer thrown from a window without warning. But first the king decided to toy with the astrologer and asked, "Tell me what your fate will be and how long you will live." Sensing a trap, the wily astrologer replied, "I shall die three days before your majesty." The king decided not to take the chance.

Reflections:

Like King Louis XI, each of us looks for a cause-effect relationship in events that we observe. In fact, you may assign causality to events that are merely coincidental. Creative people, in particular, interpret new information in terms of their causal model. Rather than change their minds, they simply ignore or distort the facts that do not fit their preconceived notions. They create their own reality. The next time you're faced with contradictory information, reexamine your assumptions.

After arriving at a conclusion, I'll retrace my steps.

"Every man has a right to his opinion, but no man has a right to be wrong in his facts."
—Bernard M. Baruch

The distinguished turn-of-the-century astronomer Percival Lowell actually wrote a book that included detailed, carefully drawn maps of 522 nonexistent Martian canals. Lowell's vision had been distorted by mistranslating the work of Italian astronomer Giovanni Schiaparelli. When Schiaparelli described *canali*, he meant channels, not canals. But having misread *canali*, Lowell saw what he was looking for, not what he was looking at. Like so many of us, he read something into the details that wasn't there.

Reflections:

In examining a subject, we magnify each aspect so as to study it closely. But magnification involves distortion—things don't appear as they actually are. That is why magnifying lenses also have resolving power, the ability to distinguish between objects that appear very close. To resolve a problem, you must distinguish between the important and unimportant details, the real and the imagined. Are you distorting a problem and reading something into the picture that isn't there? One way to gain perspective is to pretend a good friend has the problem. What advice would you give him or her?

Before resolving a problem, I must determine my biases.

> "What a strange pattern the shuttle of
> life can weave."
> —Frances Marion

In the history of commerce, few merchants
guarded their trade secrets as zealously as the
Chinese silk weavers of the Sung dynasty. Introduced in 2640 b.c., silk was the original miracle fabric,
so exquisite and rare that its secret remained within
the Middle Kingdom. According to one legend, an
enterprising Indian merchant promised to marry a
Chinese princess, provided she revealed the name
of the plant from which silk was made. To his surprise, his betrothed arrived at his home wearing a
beautiful floral hat; and inside its flowers, was the
secret of silk—not plants, but silkworms.

Reflections:

Silk can be woven into tapestries of extraordi-
narily beautiful colors and designs. But if you turn
the fabric over and look at the other side, you see
that the outline is blurred and indistinct—just like
any problem viewed from the wrong angle. The silk
merchants who yearned to discover the Chinese secret viewed the problem from the wrong angle, too.
They simply assumed that silk came from a plant.
But as we've seen, the improbable is not only possible, it is often quite likely. Are you viewing your
problems from the right angle?

I have to be open-minded.

MAY 15

"Men of very high intellectual caliber are often strikingly ineffective."
—Peter Drucker

If you've been to a college reunion, you probably were surprised at what some of your classmates have done with their lives. As often as not, the student voted most likely to succeed did not, while the class clown did. Educators now believe that schoolwork measures only one part of our mental capacity. That is, it measures the left brain, which performs the logical, verbal, and mathematical functions that we rely on in school, while the right brain performs visual-spatial and intuitive functions. To be successful in life, you have to use all your mental faculties.

Reflections:

Most business problems appeal to the left side of your brain in that they involve the manipulation of words and numbers. But you can become so engrossed in the facts and figures that you ignore the bigger picture. When that happens, your ability to respond to a situation is impaired because some of your best ideas aren't logical, they're intuitive. When your powers of reasoning are stymied by a problem, try to form a mental picture of the solution.

In analyzing my problems, I have to keep the big picture in mind.

"Where all think alike, no one thinks very much."
—Walter Lippman

The best engineering minds in the nation could not find a way to bridge the wide expanse of turbulent water at Niagara Falls. Then a young boy came forward and asked, "What if . . . " What if they flew a kite trailing a thin string across the river? Once the string spanned the river, it could pull across a stronger line, and then a rope, and eventually a cable strong enough to support a suspension bridge. Like so many breakthrough concepts, this one was based on the free association of ideas in a spontaneous, playful manner. The next time you must solve a problem, ask yourself, "What if . . . ," and let your mind soar.

Reflections:

Over the years, you have probably developed a keen analytical and logical approach to problem solving; it is one of the most notable traits of a workaholic. We excel at deductive reasoning. But often we don't have all the facts we need to arrive at a conclusion. We have to use inductive reasoning to start with the known facts, ask, "What if . . . ," and allow our minds to soar.

Today I'm going to play with some problems that I haven't been able to solve by logic alone.

"Science can progress on the basis of error so long as it is not trivial."
—Albert Einstein

Far from considering himself omniscient, Einstein spent the better part of his adult life trying to disprove the results of his own thought experiments. He understood that information leads to complexity, not simplicity, so that the more we know, the more there is to question. Consider, for example, his simple, yet elegant equation, $E = mc^2$. Within those four simple characters lies a world of unfathomable complexity, of nuclear power, nuclear medicine, and the first faint glimmerings of quantum mechanics. Nothing is as simple as it seems at first.

Reflections:

Most workaholics have an in-depth knowledge of their businesses. We enjoy being the ones with all the answers. But although our facts may pass for knowledge and our logic for insight, the truth is more elusive than we suppose. No one has all the answers—to assume omniscience is the ultimate mistake. The truly successful executives are able to admit what they don't know, and surround themselves with people who are smarter.

I'm going to look beyond simplistic, pat solutions to problems.

MAY 18

"A pinch of probability is worth a pound of perhaps."
—James Thurber

If a coin is tossed, the chances of it coming up heads are fifty–fifty, yet people call heads 76 to 79 percent of the time, according to Louis D. Goodfellow of Northwestern University. Why do we favor one side over another, when both have an equal chance of winning? Since we are in the habit of saying, "Heads or tails?" the word *heads* is more likely to come to mind first, the professor believes. Something similar happens when we are calculating our odds in other situations. We assign better odds to the most salient facts.

Reflections:

Given perfect statistical information about several business ventures, your analysis may still be skewed by salience. One fact may stand out in your mind because you're more familiar with it, or because it is more dramatic, or because you learned it most recently. Whatever the case may be, you unknowingly assign that option a value other than its true numerical value. Very few business decisions are actually made by the numbers. You can bet on it.

The best way to improve my odds is to take a chance on my Higher Power.

> "When I use a word, it means just what I choose it to mean—neither more nor less."
> —Charles Lutwidge Dodgson

Charles Lutwidge Dodgson, a leading nineteenth-century logician, considered his master work to be a book entitled *Symbolic Logic*. But he is best remembered today for writing another book, which stood logic on its head, a book of riddles, paradoxes, and imaginative *non sequiturs*. That book, written under the pen name of Lewis Carroll, was *The Adventures of Alice in Wonderland*.

Reflections:

Dodgson must have understood the limits of logic in problem solving, something we workaholics have trouble grasping. "For the sake of argument," we expect others to accept our premises and follow our logic to the obvious conclusion. But quite often other people do not accept our premises, and our conclusions do not seem as obvious to them as to us. We end up arguing for the sake of arguing.

I'm going to avoid confrontations and arguments.

"There are no facts, only interpretations."

—Friedrich Nietzsche

For many problems, there is more than one solution, but—paradoxically—these can be the most difficult problems to solve, especially if you are a workaholic. In your impatience, you may favor a trial-and-error approach, which is inappropriate when there are many alternatives and the stakes are high. You may gloss over contradictory facts and make sweeping statements leading to a pat, unimaginative solution. The richness and complexity of these problems calls for a well-considered problem-solving strategy.

Reflections:

When dealing with a problem that involves a lot of information and a number of possible solutions, you have to think methodically. In collecting your facts, look for similar situations that you can model in finding a solution. Work in collaboration with others who can broaden your view of the subject and put a different interpretation on the facts. In analyzing your options, consider combining several of them. Often the best solution to a complex problem is a compromise.

If my facts are twisted, I can't think straight.

MAY 21

"There is no data on the future."
—Laurel Cutler

Nothing rattles a workaholic like having to admit, "I don't know." Unfortunately, life is full of uncertainty. Facts do not come neatly packaged and labeled as "major premise" and "minor premise." Events occur in random, episodic order, without regard to relevance and the only thing certain about some problems is that we're not certain of anything.

Reflections:

When you're puzzled by a problem, it helps to think backward from the solution to the confusion. Ask yourself what outcome would satisfy you, and keep that big picture in mind as you examine the details. Try to impose some semblance of order—any arrangement is better than none. Externalize the problem by using numbers or symbols so you can manipulate your ideas. You don't need all the details to see the big picture. But you must reason by analogy to learn from similar situations—solutions that prove that you've had the answer all along, buried in your subconscious.

I have to put more faith in my intuition.

MAY 22

"An idea is a feat of association."
—Robert Frost

Our ability to solve certain types of problems does not depend on how far ahead we plan. Rather, it depends on the range of the ideas we consider at each step. For example, a chess master and an average player both consider thirty to fifty pieces to a depth of two to three moves each. But the chess master has a much greater range of moves from which to choose. In fact, studies by H. A. Simon and K. Gilmartin show that chess masters have a repertoire of between 10,000 and 100,000 moves.

Reflections:

If you find yourself in a competitive situation, it's best to concentrate on the next two to three steps. It's senseless to think further ahead because you can't predict your opponent's countermoves. By concentrating on the next few steps, you can put all your creative energy into generating a wider range of alternatives to the immediate problem. At each step, choose the one move with the smallest downside risk. This conservative strategy may not seem very aggressive to a red-blooded workaholic, but according to game theory it increases your chances of winning in the long run.

In solving problems, the best strategy is to proceed one step at a time.

"According to a study of unsuccessful executives, inability to make decisions is one of the principal reasons for failure."

—Herman W. Steinkrauis

In chess, white plays first, a tactical advantage worth twenty seven points. In business, the advantage lies with those who seize the initiative, too. But in planning several moves ahead, the solution to one problem seems to be another set of problems. For example, closing an unprofitable plant saves money, but it may also cost jobs, create bad publicity, lead to a boycott, lower sales, and so on. The further out you project, the larger the cumulative effect of these new problems, and the greater the likelihood you'll do nothing. In chess, the players also plan two and three moves ahead, but they have a time limit.

Reflections:

Are you stymied by a problem because every solution poses a new set of problems that seem larger than the first? Maybe you're trying to anticipate and control too many things. At the same time, you may be underestimating the risks of delay. Most problems don't go away on their own. The longer you delay in solving them, the more intractable they become, and the more drastic the solution you must implement. It's your move.

Procrastination is a risky strategy.

MAY 24

*"The people who are most likely to fail
never seem to have enough information."*
—David Viscott, M.D.

How do you fold your arms—left arm over right,
or vice versa? Most of have been folding our arms
the same way since childhood. We don't realize it
until someone asks us to fold our arms the other
way. It feels awkward and uncomfortable, doesn't it?
Something similar happens when we wrap our arms
around a problem, too. We have a natural problem-
solving style that feels right to us. But many problems cannot be solved logically because some key
information is missing; they must be solved intui-
tively.

Reflections:

Every good manager lacks one thing: enough information to prove he or she is right. All decisions
involve some doubt, or they wouldn't be decisions,
they'd be foregone conclusions. At some level, we
must rely on intuition to arrive at breakthrough
ideas. For a logical, rational workaholic, that's a tall
order. But the good news is that cognitive scientists
say we can improve our intuitive abilities. To develop your intuition, start listening to your hunches,
write them down; later, check to see whether you
were right.

*An answer doesn't have to sound logical to make
sense.*

"To have doubted one's own first principles is the mark of a civilized man."
—Oliver Wendell Holmes

In his classic text, *The Art of Clear Thinking*, Rudolf Flesch writes that most of us act as though having an open mind means sticking to our opinions and letting other people stick to theirs. However, open-mindedness actually means a willingness to accept new ideas and reject the old on the basis of new evidence. Since changing our mind is tantamount to changing ourselves, open-mindedness calls for courage and humility.

Reflection.:

Most management books state that the ability to make up your mind is a necessary attribute for success. But the ability to change your mind is equally important. Yes, it can be humbling to admit you were wrong, but the sooner an error is corrected the less humbling it is. Successful executives make as many, or more, errors as others; they're just quicker to recognize and correct their mistakes.

The only serious mistake is the one I refuse to admit.

MAY 26

*"The only thing worse than a bad deci-
sion is indecision."*

—Ray E. Brown

Johann Gutenberg never made money on his invention of movable type. He labored for years, refin-
ing and improving his device, at great expense to
himself and his financial backers. But Gutenberg
was never satisfied, and the costs rose inexorably, to
the great consternation of his investors. Finally one
investor recognized the problem was not the invention, but the inventor: Gutenberg was a procrastina-
tor. Since the investor was also a lawyer, he drew
up a contract binding Gutenberg to a firm delivery
date; and when that deadline wasn't met, all rights
to the invention reverted to the lawyer.

Reflections:

Gutenberg was overwhelmed by the enormity of
the task he had set for himself, a predicament in
which many workaholics find themselves. The result can be a form of frenetic procrastination in
which activity is confused with productivity. If you
find yourself procrastinating, break your problem
down into smaller steps, set a date for completion,
and create a time line with checkpoints for monitoring your progress. Reward yourself in some small
way each time you reach a milestone.

*If stymied by a problem, I'll break it down into
smaller steps.*

"Doubt is not a pleasant mental state,
but certainty is a ridiculous one."
—Voltaire

Many daily papers are now composed on computer screens where each type font consists of electronic dots called *pixels*. By adding or subtracting pixels, the operator can condense, italicize, flex, and stretch the letters. But throughout the changes, the mind persists in seeing the alphabet pattern. An "A" is an "A" whether it is set in Helvetica or Garamond. In a sense, we cling to our image of reality the same way—the mind simply fills in the pixels in our imagination, and we see what we expect to see.

Reflectins:

In the heading for this section, the word *Reflections* is misspelled, but most people fill in the missing "i" as if it were a pixel, and move on. These mental leaps are common among workaholics because we abhor the ambiguity of missing information. We assume that we know all the important facts and that if we don't know something, it can't be important. The result is often gibberish, or what old-time linotype operators called ETAOIN SHRDLU.

Before leaping to a conclusion, I will verify my facts.

"Tomorrow is often the busiest day of the year."

—Spanish proverb

London's Royal Society, the oldest and most famous scientific society in the world, has as its motto, *"Nullius in verba,"* which means, "Don't take anybody's word for it." Like every good scientist, workaholics are naturally skeptical, but our endless factfinding can be a form of procrastination. If all our facts were laid end to end, they wouldn't come to a conclusion; only we can do that when we venture out beyond the shoreline of knowledge.

Reflections:

One symptom of procrastination is a feverish "busyness." We overprepare for meetings, do things that could be easily delegated or automated, and allow low-priority projects to disrupt our work load. We become preoccupied with procedure instead of progress. We start second-guessing others and making excuses for ourselves. The next time you find yourself missing deadlines, ask yourself what you're trying to avoid.

I am going to embrace today's problems with enthusiasm.

"One of these days is none of these days."

—English proverb

A workaholic sales rep was always too busy making his next sales call to handle his paperwork. Finally, the home office sent a letter saying it could not fill his latest order until he submitted the paperwork. The sales rep wired back, "Please cancel order—customer can't wait that long." Why is it that some of us are always running behind?

Reflections:

Some people procrastinate because they think it puts them in a win-win situation. Given the shortness of time, they feel that if they succeed they look like heroes; and if they lose, no one would blame them, given the circumstances. But once you start to procrastinate you set a dangerous precedent in that people soon begin to expect the impossible of you on short notice. In procrastinating, you don't give yourself enough time to do your best, so you might fail. In either case putting it off leaves you in a high-stress position. Give yourself firm deadlines and stick to them.

I'm going to put due dates next to each project on my "To Do" list.

*"Whether you believe you can do a thing
or not, you are right."*

—Henry Ford

Henry Ford founded and failed at two other auto companies before launching Ford Motor Company at age forty. In both cases, his setbacks were due to Ford's constant tinkering with the auto's design, which led to numerous production and delivery problems. Ford seems to have had the same problem that many workaholics have: a fear of failure that leads to an obsession with details, a loss of perspective and unfocused activity. The breakthrough in Ford's thinking came when he realized he was thinking too small. "The proper system, as I have it in mind," he said, "is to get the car to the multitudes."

Reflections:

Mass production was well established in U.S. industry before Henry Ford hit on the idea. It was already being used to produce Singer sewing machines, McCormick reapers, Colt firearms, and Oldsmobile cars. But after two failures Ford realized the error of his ways. Once he began thinking on a big scale, the moving assembly line followed, and the course of manufacturing changed forever. If you find yourself tinkering with a problem, and getting hung up on details, start thinking bigger.

I have to keep the big picture in mind.

MAY 31

*"It's hard to detect good luck—it looks
so much like something you've earned."*
—Frank A. Clark

Everyday reality confronts us with events that,
on the surface, seem improbable simply because we
are not fluent in probability theory. For example,
when you are waiting for an elevator your intuition
might say there is a fifty-fifty chance that the next
elevator would go up. But in *Aha! Gotcha!* Martin
Gardner points out the odds depend on whether the
floor you're waiting on is above or below the halfway point in the building. The higher up you are
the less chance there is of an elevator above you and
going down, and the greater the chance of an elevator below you coming up.

Reflections:

Most people spend their whole lives waiting for
an "up" elevator. When things go their way, they
assume they were smart enough to hit the right button. But when the elevator drops, they attribute it to
bad luck, poor timing, the breaks. If things aren't
going your way, make your own breaks by taking the
stairway. Your odds of getting an up elevator increase with every flight up. You can recognize the
door to the stairway because the sign above it reads
"opportunity."

*To create my own opportunity, I have to step out in
faith.*

JUNE

Aggression

The strain to maintain control of an unrealistic work load and our frustrated ambitions can make us hostile and aggressive. Our competitive approach may have contributed to early career success, but if our combativeness isn't kept in check it eventually becomes self-defeating. We have to make amends to those we've attacked and ask God to transform our character defects.

JUNE 1

"There is no failure except in no longer trying."

—Elbert Hubbard

The three most competitive words in the English language are "request for proposals"—the bidding process, when businesses go head to head and the winner takes all. No matter how good you are, someone, sometime, is going to outbid you. How you deal with the frustration and disappointment of losing determines, to a large degree, your true success. Do you become angry and cynical, or do you put the loss behind you and tackle the next proposal as a great opportunity? Do you feel envious, or do you learn from the experience and go on? Is somebody outbidding you for your happiness?

Reflections:

A cynic once said, "Show me a good loser, and I'll show you a loser." But if you expect to win all the time, you're sure to lose. The real winners recognize that they are going to get their share of wins and losses. When they lose, they put the past behind them and focus on the present opportunities, determined to win. They greet each new business presentation with enthusiasm, and their outlook affects the outcome.

Win or lose, I'm grateful for the opportunity to compete.

JUNE 2

"Every great man of business has got somewhere a touch of the idealist in him."

—Woodrow Wilson

Under Darwinian economics, survival of the fittest seems to favor the most competitive. But, in actuality, head-to-head competition is a costly strategy leading to a diversion of scarce resources to nonproductive purposes. Its weakness can be seen in companies that rely on sales promotions and price cuts, only to lose market share. The real business lesson of the "descent of man" is that success belongs to those that adapt to their environment rather than struggle against it.

Reflections:

Of all the adaptive strategies nature has evolved, one of the most effective is symbiosis, or cooperation among species. Birds flock, fish school, and hoofed animals herd because cooperation is usually more advantageous than competition. Only humankind among the communal species is so competitive. We assume that competition is a way of life and that our job is to beat the other person, even if he or she works for our company! However, in business, as in nature, the most rewarding strategy may be cooperation.

Sometimes I have to go along to get along.

"We have met the enemy and he is us."
—Walt Kelly

According to biologist Gierat J. Verney, competition among species is often self-defeating. As evolution escalates, he says, the environment becomes more rigorous because other species also adapt to survive. Any advantage is short-lived and increasingly costly to maintain. The most successful species have allies, either other offspring or other species with which a symbiotic relationship is established. In effect, cooperation is their competitive strategy.

Reflections:

To compete, many successful companies establish strategic alliances or cooperative efforts. High-tech manufacturers rely on independent software developers, makers of peripheral equipment, dealers, and retailers. Automotive companies like Ford and Mazda, Chrysler and Mitsubishi, form joint ventures. Major airlines link up to travel agents by computer. Banks use automated teller networks. Business imitates nature, and people within businesses must do the same. Is there someone at work who could use your help? Are you cooperating as much as you should?

Today I'm going to be more helpful to co-workers.

JUNE 4

"Almost every company does better if it has a single competitor to focus on."
—John Sculley

John Sculley became the consummate competitor at Pepsi Cola and at Apple Computer. But he now believes that it is more important to create than compete. As he puts it, "I've also discovered a new world where ... success is measured, not by share points, but by enlarging the playing field for everyone." What about you? Are you fighting battles on every front, or, have you channeled some of your competitive drive into creating new business opportunities?

Reflections:

Competition is inevitable. But the prudent executive views competition as wasteful and tries to minimize it. Focusing on a single competitor instead of many, is more efficient and more effective. It gives us a standard for measuring our performance. By contrast, people who fight on every front never get a clear sense of whether they're winning or losing. In a sense, their overly aggressive tactics mask the fact that they are unwilling to take a stand and fight for what they believe in.

The moment I take on more than one competitor, I am outnumbered.

JUNE 5

"They are able who think they are able."
—Virgil

Humorist Joe Taylor Ford tells the story of an executive whose first-grader asked him why he brought work home every night. The father explained that he had so much work to do that he couldn't finish it during the day. "Then," his son asked innocently, "why don't they just put you in a slower group?" Actually, the little boy was close to the truth. All workaholics feel at times as if they are in the "slow group." We suffer from a chronic sense of being left behind. Someone is always getting ahead of us, passing us by. We can never catch up.

Reflections:

When you think about it, someone is always getting the jump on you, and there is absolutely nothing you can do about it. While you're working overtime on your sales plan, a competitor is working on a promotion plan. While you're working on your promotion plan, he or she is working on an advertising plan. While the two of you work on your plans, another competitor is shaking hands with your customers or hiring away your best sales reps. The best you can do is the best you can do. And that's good enough.

The best I can do is the best I can do.

JUNE 6

"Success once shared is success twice earned."

—Bob Larrañaga

David Sarnoff, long-time chairman of RCA, was a pioneer in radio and color television. He was also a fiercely competitive man, who, in the words of his biographer Kenneth Bilby was "never known to weep when lesser enterprises than his were driven to the wall." At the same time, Sarnoff appreciated what could be achieved through cooperation. To assure the quality of radio broadcasts, he advocated linking stations all across the country in a network. In 1926, under Sarnoff's guidance, the National Broadcasting Company was born.

Reflections:

Often you can accomplish more through cooperation than competition. There is synergy in cooperation, which makes the sum of the parts greater than the whole. Energy wasted in contention and strife can be channeled into more productive areas for the common good. Everyone benefits when we put aside selfish interests and share our limited resources. Why not make a commitment to yourself today to start working with a friendly competitor?

I'm going to invite a competitor to lunch.

"Military intelligence is a contradiction in terms."

—Groucho Marx

The language of business is rich in military metaphors. We talk of "targeting" a market, "launching a campaign," scheduling an ad "blitz," bringing in the "big guns." We "attack" a problem, call our sales forces "the troops," and "take aim" at the competition. We describe business as though it were war—the penultimate form of competition—and act as if every share point, gain or loss, were a matter of life and death. In such fierce competition, we can mistake our free-floating hostility for a valuable weapon.

Reflections:

Do you believe success is based on "beating the other guy?" What about all those times you won through cooperation and teamwork? How many times have you pitched in to help another employee? How many times have you given a subordinate a pat on the back or an encouraging word? How often have you dropped someone a congratulatory note, or shared the credit for a successful project? And haven't other employees helped you in return? When you think about it, a lot of your success has been based on helping the other guy win, hasn't it?

I'm at my best when I'm attacking problems, not people.

JUNE 8

"All the significant battles are waged within the self."

—Sheldon Kopp

On the eve of a Civil War battle, Jefferson Davis was riding the front lines, raising the spirits of his troops. But at one outpost a young sentry called, "Halt! Who goes there?" "Jefferson Davis," he replied. A rifle cocked and a voice barked, "I said, identify yourself!" "But I am Jefferson Davis," he pleaded. Now, the sentry had never seen Davis, but one thing he knew—the president would not be on the front lines. As the sentry took aim, Davis cried out, "W-w-wait, I can prove it! See this envelope I have here in my saddlebag? Take a look at the face on the postage stamp." With that, Johnny Reb snapped to attention.

Reflections:

Most of us have been like that young sentry at times—attacking problems or people without a clear idea of what we're fighting for. We're simply angry and enjoy the sense of power our emotional outburst gives us. Before you raise your voice, use profanity and attack someone else personally, ask yourself what you're fighting for. You stand a much better chance of winning by calming down.

May I become brave enough to conquer myself.

JUNE 9

"The time to win a fight is before it starts."
—Frederick W. Lewis

Most workaholics are aggressive, attacking all problems and adversaries head on. However, it's worth noting that throughout military history very few major battles have been won by full frontal attack. According to historian B. H. Liddell Hart and Robert Heller, "From the time of ancient Greece to the First World War, out of thirty major conflicts and 280 campaigns, in only six . . . did decisive results follow from head-on assaults." More often than not, victory is won by a flanking attack.

Reflections:

To achieve anything worthwhile, you must be assertive. But, there is a difference between being assertive and being aggressive. If you meet resistance head on with a full frontal attack, if you pound tables with clenched fists, and if you use profanity to intimidate, you're aggressive. If you confront others directly, speaking freely, without attacking them personally; and if you remain poised and resolve conflicts through compromise, then you are assertive. Assertive managers outflank the competition and win more battles.

The best way to disarm an opponent is by being polite.

JUNE 10

"The best armor is to keep out of range."
—Italian proverb

In most companies, management turnover is 25 to 30 percent a year. If you work in a typical twelve-person department, there is an opening every three months, and it is another nine months before the new person is fully productive. In other words, your department is chronically understaffed, and everyone is handling more than one job. Roles become ambiguous as duties change. Political infighting reshapes organization charts. Battles for "territory" reconfigure office layouts. And personality clashes occur.

Reflections:

A change in group dynamics triggers a strong reaction in us all because a threat to our job status is a threat to ourselves. It strikes at the core of our being where we identify closely with our work. Constant turnover creates low levels of chronic stress and aggressive behavior. In a politically charged atmosphere, a confrontational style actually poses a greater threat to our job security than management turnover itself. To succeed, we must take a flexible in approach to the job.

The key duty in my job description reads, "Performs other tasks that may be assigned."

JUNE 11

"A politician is one who thinks twice before saying nothing."

—Anonymous

The political atmosphere in today's corporation virtually assures a certain amount of internal competition. We compete for funding, promotions, recognition, and perks. In such a hostile environment, it's easy to lose perspective and try to win at all costs, driving subordinates, bawling them out, and demeaning them in front of others. When something goes wrong, we may fire off accusations in every direction ("Ready, fire, aim!") only to learn that a white-hot temper draws return fire from heat-seeking memoranda that explode in mid-career.

Reflections:

Successful managers understand the importance of cooperation; instead of viewing co-workers as competitors, they see them as allies. They try to strengthen their relationships with subordinates, peers, and superiors. It may be as simple as inviting someone to lunch, going fishing or golfing together, or taking in dinner and a movie with your spouses. Are you working as hard at strengthening your relationships as you do at handling each task that crosses your desk?

My Higher Power does not choose sides; neither will I.

"Leadership is action, not position."
—Donald McGannon

The down-sizing of companies inevitably leads to role conflict. Jobs disappear; but the workload remains, and the overwhelmed employees start to set their own priorities. Factions form, and political infighting begins as first one group and then another becomes aggressive. In this situation, the advantage lies with those who recognize change is inevitable and that the work must be streamlined, functions combined. They're quick to discuss the situation with a supervisor and other employees in order to arrive at workable new procedures. In short, they cooperate.

Reflections:

This is one of those times when your aggressive workaholic style must be channeled into cooperative efforts. Role conflicts are best handled in a straightforward but tactful manner. Trying to ignore the situation only bottles up the stress you're feeling. It comes out sideways in arguments and office politics. You feel it in back spasms, migraine headaches, and other psychosomatic symptoms. You're better off dealing with the problem by asserting yourself in a calm, matter-of-fact manner.

Down-sizing creates an opportunity for me to be cooperative.

JUNE 13

"The unspoken word never defeated anyone."
—Sam Rayburn

You lend someone an important file, and he or she loses it. You give someone else a raise, and he or she tells you it isn't enough. You hit the wrong key on your computer and erase three hours of work faster than you can say "glitch." Under the circumstances, anyone might get angry. But the way you express your anger can have serious repercussions in your dealings with others. If you release a colorful stream of expletives at the nearest object or person, your hostile behavior is self-defeating.

Reflections:

Contrary to popular belief, venting your anger may not be cathartic. If you shout and curse, you legitimize and reinforce negative feelings. Long after the incident has passed, your words echo in the recesses of your mind, beyond the reach of Anacin. You may experience guilt and anxiety over what you said in rage. Worse, your words also echo in the minds of those you attacked. A curse hurled at a co-worker kills the spirit of friendship as surely as any weapon. Is there someone at work you need to make amends to today?

In guarding my tongue, I protect my reputation.

JUNE 14

"Be careful of your thoughts; they may become words at any moment."
—Iara Gassen

Do you harbor grudges? When another employee does something to irritate you, do you take it personally and look for ways to get even? There are few heavier burdens than the grudges we bear. They weigh us down with resentments, bitterness, and heaviness of heart. We can feel the strain in our neck, shoulder muscles, and back. Our anger can inflict more physical harm on us than we ever experienced at the hands of the person who provoked us.

Reflections:

Letting go of our anger and our need for revenge isn't easy, but regular exercise helps release the tension that builds up in the course of a stressful day. To get some of the exercise you need, consider parking your car a few blocks from the office, use the stairs instead of the elevator and walk instead of taking a cab to close-by business appointments. Of course, it makes sense to consult your doctor before beginning a more vigorous exercise program.

Letting go of my desire for revenge is a gift I give myself.

JUNE 15

"When angry, count to four; when very angry, swear."

—Mark Twain

When you suppress your anger, it comes out sideways, sometimes when you least expect it. It may be expressed long after the fact, and, worse, behind the other person's back. In any case, you probably expect the person to whom you complain to relay your comment to the other person. You're avoiding a confrontation in which you might lose emotional control because you don't trust your own feelings. You don't know what you might say in the heat of the moment.

Reflections:

Your anger needs healthy expression. It need not be shouted, and it definitely should not involve backbiting. Claim your feelings and state, "This is how I feel . . . " It's an authentic expression of who you are. Be honest, direct, and assertive. Avoid attacking the person. Focus on his or her behavior. Resist the temptation to transfer the hurt you're feeling to the other person. That's not the outcome you want, because it merely assures that he or she will disown the problem. The other person needs to know what would please you. So what outcome do you want?

If I lose control of my temper, I lose.

"When a man points a finger at someone else, he should remember that four of his fingers are pointing at him."
—Louis Nizer

Anger can be a way to avoid responsibility for our own mistakes. By blaming our subordinates, we can act superior and absolve ourselves of any wrongdoing. The temptation to shift blame can be very strong in workaholics who are perfectionists. In order to live with our unrealistic expectations, we may look for a scapegoat when things go wrong. In our anger, we may attack them in public and use sarcasm and profanity to belittle them. And all the while the real cause of the problem may be ourselves.

Reflections:

One thing you can be certain of is that the person you criticized does not like being pilloried in public. Immobilized by your anger, confidence shaken, that person resents your actions and will avoid you. Without that person's cooperation, the problem that triggered your outburst can worsen. Maybe it's time you took a closer look at your role in this situation. Everyone makes mistakes. By admitting yours, you may restore your co-worker's faith in you.

I have to accept responsibility for my part in any problem!

JUNE 17

> "Winning isn't everything. It's the only thing."
> —Vince Lombardi, former coach of the Green Bay Packers

When it comes to winning, most workaholics share Vince Lombardi's management philosophy. But, unlike football, life is not a zero-sum game in which my gain is your loss and *vice versa*. We can both win. Lombardi himself later added, "I wish to hell I'd never said the damned thing. I meant having a goal. . . . I sure as hell didn't mean for people to crush human values and morality."

Reflections:

We workaholics have to learn to control our competitive drive, which can lead to aggressive, even hostile, behavior toward co-workers. A discussion can quickly become an argument because our competitive nature prompts us to question, comment, and complain. Instead of competing with your co-workers, support their efforts, make allowances for their work styles, and cooperate whenever possible. One sure way to promote cooperation is to ask someone for help.

I can accomplish more by working through others than working around them.

"You cannot shake hands with a clenched fist."

—Indira Gandhi

A clenched fist is only good for one thing—fighting. It can't lift; it can't pat; it can't stroke or squeeze; it can't push or pull; it can't reach out to others for help. When we constantly fight with co-workers, we clench inside, lose our spontaneity and our creativity. We become too defensive to recognize and grasp opportunities that are within our reach.

Reflections:

When things go wrong, are you more intent on fixing the blame than fixing the problem? Do you strike out at others, and criticize and demean them for mistakes? A Columbia University study showed that when people were criticized in private, 66 percent improved; when they were ridiculed in public, only 34 percent improved. Another group of workers were praised before being criticized in private, and 88 percent improved. One of the great lessons in life is that no one does it alone; we need one another to succeed. Is there someone at work who could use a friendly gesture, a helping hand, or a pat on the back from you? Is there someone whose offer of help you have spurned?

Today I will extend myself to someone else, asking nothing in return.

JUNE 19

*"Tact is the art of making your point
without making an enemy."*
—Howard W. Newton

The favorite word in a workaholic's vocabulary
is *but*. Our confrontational nature leads us to interrupt, discount, or object to other viewpoints and
qualify every statement. If a supervisor asks our
opinion, we may feign agreement by saying, "You're
right," only to follow up with, "but ... " If we're
asked to defend our own performance, we might
say, "Sure, it came in over budget, but ... ," then
justify ourselves. And if we're asked to appraise a
subordinate, we inevitably give qualified praise, as
in, "Terrific job, but next time ... " The word *but* is
a red flag to anyone who works with us.

Reflections:

Given the competitive nature of work, a certain
amount of confrontation is inevitable. You can minimize the number of heated discussions you're involved in by avoiding the word *but*. As Anthony
Robbins points out in *Unlimited Power*, you can
usually substitute the word *and* for *but* and make
your point more effectively because the other person
is not put on the defensive.

*I'm going to be less confrontational—no ifs, ands, or
buts about it.*

JUNE 20

"If you want someone to hang on your every world, repeat what they just said."
—Bob Larrañaga

The no-nonsense factual approach that workaholics take to life can create problems in a business relationship. In many working sessions, it is not the facts that are in dispute, but rather the way people feel about the facts. By focusing on the literal facts, we can completely miss the emotional message sent by the other person. When that happens, a dispute is inevitable.

Reflections:

In an argument, the natural tendency is to go on the offensive and question, challenge, and complain. But these tactics simply exacerbate the situation. A more effective approach would be to clarify how others feel about the facts by restating their position. Once they sense that you respect their feelings; they'll be more inclined to hear what you have to say, too. Mutual respect will eventually lead to agreement.

The harder I listen, the better I'm heard.

"It's easier to fight for one's principles
than live up to them."

—Alfred Adler

Dick Knowlton, chairman of Geo. A. Hormel,
faced a crisis when a renegade union struck the
company's meat-packing plant. Knowlton had been
a boyhood friend of some of the picketers who now
confronted him in a bitter strike that threatened Hormel's survival. The media baited him, pickets be-
rated him, and outside agitators vilified him. But
Knowlton didn't let his personal feelings color his
thinking. "I refused to be reactionary," he says.
Within ten months, he not only settled the strike on
Hormel's terms but also increased sales 34 percent.
As a result, Dick Knowlton won the Carnegie Mellon
Crisis Management Award.

Reflections:

The normal tendency when you're unjustly attacked is to counterattack with all you can muster.
But that merely escalates hostilities. In dealing with
criticism, establish rapport; listen to the people on
the other side and show respect for their position.
Disarm them by agreeing on inconsequential points.
Tactfully yet assertively state your position on key
points. It worked for Knowlton, and it can work for
you.

To be credible, I must be truthful. And, above all, I
must be true to myself.

"Power is no more than winning."
—Roy Ash

As a workaholic, your natural style is to attack a problem head on, with all the intellectual firepower you can muster. Your formidable powers of concentration and persistence often overcome the difficulties you encounter in the normal course of events. But at times an aggressive, forceful approach can be self-defeating. Sometimes you can accomplish more by being flexible and avoiding conflict.

Reflections:

Each of us handles conflict in our own way. Some might roll up their sleeves and go right to work; others might close one eye to the situation and see if it goes away; still others might chain-smoke and fret their way to a solution. We combat, or we capitulate, or we cope. Can you think of a situation when you increased your stress by being too forceful? Have there been times when you overreacted to a challenge, making the situation worse? Or have you bottled up your anger only to explode at an inopportune moment? As you think back over the conflicts you encountered this past week, and knowing what you know now, would you have reacted differently to them?

I need to be more flexible in my approach to problem solving.

"All life is an experiment."
　　　　—Ralph Waldo Emerson

Management consultant Fred Pryor observes that it is difficult to get people to change, but comparatively easy to get them to "experiment." Change connotes irrevocability, whereas an "experiment" is controlled, of limited duration, and implies an open-minded, wait-and-see attitude on the part of management. It suggests that management has more questions than answers and is looking to the staff for input. The staff has a hand in the experiment, and, as such, they are empowered by it, rather than threatened by it.

Reflections:

We workaholics are change agents, always stirring things up, revising organization charts, redefining objectives and goals. So long as we are the ones causing the changes, we feel as if we are in control. But in our zeal to prove that we're the boss and in charge, we fail to see how our changes might be seen by others. We just assume the wisdom of our decisions is apparent to all, and we move forward in our initiatives without considering how others might interpret them. Is there someone whose input you should get on a new project?

I must be more experimental and involve others in my projects.

*"Anxiety in human life is what squeak-
ing and grinding are in machinery that
is not oiled. In life, trust is the oil."*
—Henry Ward Beecher

One of your most distinguishing characteristics
is your self-reliance. But doing everything by yourself can lead to a feeling that it's "you against the
world." Those are pretty overwhelming odds! It
wouldn't be surprising for you to inwardly rail
against the unfairness of life. In a state of chronic
hostility, your body produces abnormal amounts of
adrenalin, higher levels of cholesterol, and raised
blood pressure. It must seem that the only way to
release the pressure welling up inside you is an outburst of anger.

Reflections:

Do you feel as though you are all alone, overworked, and downright angry? If you lose your temper now, you may lose a friend when you need one
the most. Doctors say that the people best able to
cope with job stress are those with strong support
systems. Friends, co-workers, family, and relatives
help us keep things in perspective. Is there someone
at work with whom you can share your feelings before you lose your temper?

*When I don't trust my own reactions, I need a friend
I can trust.*

"Every company has its quota of executives who judge the value of what they have to say by the number of people who are forced to listen. For these executives, an important meeting is one in which there aren't enough chairs to go around."

—Mark McCormack

As a company grows and becomes more departmentalized, the number of meetings also grows, which places greater emphasis on your ability to communicate in a group. We workaholics have a tendency to dominate meetings. We squelch good ideas by hurrying the comments of others. We nod pneumatically and say "yes . . . yes"; we interrupt, finish sentences and act as if others had nothing important to say. We doodle, drum our fingers and squirm in our chair until everyone else is uncomfortable. If this sounds familiar, you'd better review your performance in meetings.

Reflections:

There are several steps you can take to make sure your meetings run smoothly. First, send out a memo in advance stating the purpose of the meeting, the agenda and the starting and ending time. Attach to the memo any pertinent background information and make it clear that each participant's opinions are valued. Once the meeting starts, stick to the agenda, encourage everyone to talk while you listen attentively.

Listening solves more problems than talking.

"Never forget what a man says when he's angry."

—Henry Ward Beecher

Everybody who has ever lost his or her temper has said, "I couldn't stop myself." One reason why it is difficult to control anger is that expressing it feels so "right" at the time. Self-righteousness is a component of much of anger. We feel we have been wronged and that we are entitled to retribution. So we attack and verbally abuse the other person in order to redress the grievance.

Reflections:

Anger is often the precursor of a desire for revenge. Ironically, the person who pays the most is the one seeking revenge. We do ourselves more harm than the other person ever did by replaying the original incident in our minds, over and over again. Each time we think about it, we inflict on ourselves painful memories that stir the subconscious and our nervous system, as if the event were happening again. We wouldn't accept such treatment from anyone else, yet we do it to ourselves all the time.

Forgiveness is a gift I give myself.

"No man fails who does his best."
—Orison Suett Marden

Sooner or later we all have a "run of bad luck," when the breaks don't go our way. We may lose out on a big contract or be assigned to a job we don't like or to a boss who doesn't like us. The sheer grinding frustration of the position can have a greater cumulative effect on our well-being than a major crisis. On the trip home at night, as we replay the events of the day, our emotions shift into fast forward, and by the time we reach home we're screaming inside like an audio cassette playing at the wrong speed.

Reflections:

The first three minutes after entering the house set the tone for the rest of the night. When you stand in the entranceway and say through gritted teeth, "I hate my job," don't be surprised if you get a cool reception. Your angry outburst can spark resentment in a spouse who feels victimized by your rage and unable to help you solve your problem. If possible, take your mind off work long enough to put things in proper perspective. Wait until after dinner to calmly discuss your day at the office.

I'm going to limit my table talk to family matters, rather than business.

JUNE 28

"It takes all the running you can do to keep in the same place. If you want to get somewhere else, you must run at least twice as fast."
—Alice in *Through the Looking Glass*,
by Lewis Carroll

You run all day at top speed, and at night you collapse, exhausted, into the easy chair in front of the television set. It's time to relax. But when you hit the remote control button, the screen mirrors all the problems you thought you had left at the office. Leveraged buyouts, spinoffs, shutdowns, trade wars, and economic upheaval: in thirty minutes of high-compression video, all your business problems flash before your eyes. Your mind races to keep up with them, and although it is bedtime you cannot sleep.

Reflections:

The television screen is a looking glass of flickering images that mirror the changes taking place in your world. Many of the news reports have no direct bearing on your life, but your mind takes them all in as if they were relevant. At night, your subconscious wrestles with this news and tries to make sense of it. Instead of feeling relaxed, you feel restless and assaulted. No wonder you're tired and hostile.

Rather than watch television, I'll listen to music or read a book.

JUNE 29

"In the scale of destinies, brawn will never weigh so much as brain."
—James Russell Lowell

Episodes of workaholism are frequently tied to business cycles such as the end of the month when you have to make quota, close out the books, or count inventory. At such times there are more projects on your calendar than hours in the day. Your only meaningful conversations are with your dictating machine, and the night table next to your bed looks like your "in" basket. Under the pressure to perform, you can become irritable and hostile.

Reflections:

Knowing when the work load pressures increase can help you prepare in advance. Try to schedule your time in such a way as to allow for relaxing, leisure activities. Include some stress-relieving stretching exercises, and guard against the tendency to overeat so you'll feel "big enough" to handle your problems. By pacing yourself, you can cope with the frustrations that trigger feelings of hostility.

Easy does it.

JUNE 30

"Logic is the art of going wrong with confidence."
—Joseph Wood Krutch

Maybe you don't fit the stereotype image of a two-fisted, domineering workaholic. Maybe you don't pound tables and shout. But your aggression can take other forms, some so subtle that you may not be aware of them yourself. It could be as "innocent" as giving someone a nickname, or as cutting as a sarcastic joke. Or it might be as serious as leaving someone's name off a routing list, or not inviting them to a meeting. Whatever the form, that is passive aggression.

Reflections:

The trouble with passive aggression is that it looks so much like good, sound management. It seems so logical. After all, you're supposed to be on a first-name basis with your staff, so what harm can a nickname do? Everyone knows you need a good sense of humor to handle this job. And as for that routing list—hey, we have too many people on this project team already, right? Not necessarily. You may be simply avoiding dealing with the underlying causes of your anger. What's really bothering you?

It takes a small-minded person to belittle someone else.

JULY

Critical Thinking

Our rigid style of thinking can make us intolerant of others' mistakes. When something goes wrong, we're quick to fix the blame instead of fixing the problem. When we make a mistake, rather than admit it, we blame someone else. Our superior attitude drives out competent people, and we become surrounded by sycophants and politicians. We need the humility to admit when we're wrong.

*"Man is a creature who spends his entire
life trying to convince himself that he is
not absurd."*

—Albert Camus

We workaholics pride ourselves on being logical. But frequently we rationalize and use logic to
justify our preconceived notions. Those who dis-
agree with us are censored and made to appear foolish. If your subordinates agree with you on every
issue, it could be that they have learned it doesn't
pay to argue with you. You have an answer for
everything, and sometimes the answer wounds their
pride.

Reflections:

Goethe said, "When an idea is wanting, a word
can always be found to take its place." The next time
a staff member disagrees with you, resist the temptation to interrupt and rebut; simply remain silent,
nodding your understanding while he or she talks.
Suspend judgment until after you've had a chance
to think through what you want to say. Avoid being
critical. Without an open exchange of ideas, there
can be no flash of insight, no breakthrough thinking.

*I need to encourage my staff members to express
their views.*

"The Devil is the oldest friend of insight."

—Friedrich Nietzsche

A strong need for control leads to skepticism and a questioning of others. But there is no end to the questions you might ask, because knowledge does not lead to certitude—the more you learn, the more you realize there is to learn. A critical, dialectical management style may or may not spark insight, but it can definitely spark conflict with coworkers. Caught off guard by your questions, they may feel foolish, and suspect that you enjoy their discomfort and the sense of power it brings you. Sadly, they may be right.

Reflections:

Questions can be a powerful communications tool, provided your line of questioning is clear to the other person and doesn't threaten them. Good questioners state the outcome they're looking for and ask only those questions that can fill in the gaps in that picture. The situation is analogous to putting the pieces of a puzzle together—it's easier when you know what the puzzle looks like. Before questioning someone else, question yourself about the outcome you want.

I can learn more by asking fewer, more directed questions.

JULY 3

"It is better to debate a question without settling it than to settle a question without debating it."

—Joseph Joubert

Due to your natural skepticism, your mode of inquiry can be like that of a lawyer cross-examining a witness. Lawyers never ask a question unless they already know the answer—they lead the witness, and that's the same impression you may create at times. Instead of asking open-ended questions to draw other people out, you look for gaps in their thinking, flaws in their logic. In the end, they may feel vulnerable, as if caught in a game of "Gotcha," and may resist sharing information with you.

Reflections:

The role of a devil's advocate can be invaluable in thinking through a complex problem. But in many business situations there is not one right answer. You can probe, but you cannot prove. On some level, your thinking is subject to the laws of fractal geometry: the closer you examine a subject, the more facets you see and the more complex it becomes. It's important to recognize that the other person may be focusing on a different facet of the problem. There may not be a simple answer.

I don't have all the questions, much less all the answers.

JULY 4

"Knowledge isn't the end. It's a beginning, a jumping off point."
—Bill Bernbach

Ad man Bill Bernbach told of traveling in winter to a small midwestern town to visit one of his clients. Arriving at night and chilled to the bone, he decided to have a bowl of soup in the hotel restaurant. "What is the soup du jour?" he asked the young waitress. "Gee," she said, "I don't know. I'm new here. But I'll ask the chef." Moments later, the waitress returned and, beaming, announced, "The chef says the *soup du jour* is 'the soup of the day.'" The point of Bernbach's story: the way you ask a question determines the answer you get.

Reflections:

Communication is a process of discovery in which our questions draw the other person out. Workaholics tend to ask directed questions and probing questions. They require a choice of alternatives ("Which do you prefer . . . ?") or force the other person to justify an opinion ("Why did you . . . ?"). Both types of questions create a defensive mood and stifle communication. To learn more, ask open-ended questions ("What do you think . . . ?") and hypothetical questions ("What if . . . ?").

In asking questions, I'll give others benefit of the doubt.

JULY 5

"The older I grow, the more I listen to people who don't say much."
—Germaine G. Glidden

Chances are, in the course of your work, other people solicit your approval, ask your opinion, and follow your instructions to the letter. It can be a pretty heady experience—feeling "infallible." If you're not careful, you may begin to monopolize the conversation, interrupt others, and speak patronizingly. We workaholics can excel at the penetrating one-liner, but in the process we sacrifice good two-way communication with our co-workers.

Reflections:

The wonder is that we can communicate at all. The five hundred most commonly used words have 14,000 definitions, and no word has exactly the same meaning for two people because each person has a unique perspective. To improve communication with your co-workers, ask open-ended questions and listen intently until they're finished speaking. Avoid loaded questions and an overemphasis on "why." Rather than summarize a conversation, ask other people to do so. You'll not only make them feel important because they have the final say, you'll also learn whether or not you're communicating.

I will try to ask more questions than are asked of me.

JULY 6

"No one means all he says and yet very few say all they mean."
—Henry Adams

Our system of written communication represents the sounds of words rather than their meaning as in the more symbolic ideographic Chinese and Egyptian style. As a result, our communication is burdened by more rules of grammar, such as tense of verbs and gender of nouns. According to Rudolf Flesch, the complexity of our rules places more emphasis on form and less emphasis on content. At the same time, the rules introduce artificial distinctions in our very thought processes. Without realizing it, we become more discerning and judgmental because our words shape our thoughts as much as our thoughts shape our words.

Reflections:

Our writing system makes us prone to classify, distinguish, and note differences. It makes us critical of those who don't think as we do. The more verbally fluent and discerning we become, the more likely we are to be judgmental of others. However, truly gifted managers look for points in common with their co-workers, rather than points of difference.

If I have offended others with my sharp tongue, I'll apologize.

JULY 7

"Write down the thought of the moment. Those that come unsought for are commonly the most valuable."
—Francis Bacon

One of the creators of the mathematical theory of information, Claude Shannon of AT&T, made an interesting distinction between information and noise. Information, he said, can only be transmitted when the signal contains a predictable pattern of on-off pulses, as opposed to a continuous hum. According to Shannon, the pauses between signals buffer the information. By analogy, we need periodic breaks in the stream of information crossing our desks so we can process, analyze, and absorb what we have read. Otherwise, all information becomes noise.

Reflections:

The signs of information overload range from memory lapses and missed appointments to an over-reliance on "top-line numbers" without a clear understanding of how the figures were derived. But the real cost of information overload is less obvious. Without time to reflect on the information crossing your desk, you lose touch with your subconscious ability to filter the noise from the signals. Your whole life is filled with static. Give yourself quiet time at the beginning and end of each day to reflect on what you've read.

I need at least half an hour each day to hear myself think.

"The incessant production of new data
and its instantaneous communication
create a paradox: information, the thing
that eliminates uncertainty, now increases everybody's feeling of insecurity because of the failure to convert data into
knowledge."
—Walter Wriston, former chairman of
the board of Citicorp

At the periphery of conscious thought, we are
always on the verge of information overload: there
are too many sensory inputs to process. So we subconsciously screen out some part of every moment
and live with the uncertainty that we may have overlooked some vital piece of information.

Reflections:

It's easy to get lost in the maze of information
that crosses our desk each day as we anxiously
search for solutions. But often the simplest solution
is the best one. For example, to find your way out of
a maze, one need only keep one hand on a wall at
all times, and eventually you'll reach the exit. Sim-
ilarly, we workaholics have to keep walking in the
direction of recovery, one step at a time.

*The only thing I'm certain about is I want to lead a
balanced life.*

JULY 9

"One machine can do the work of 50 ordinary men. No machine can do the work of one extraordinary man."
　　　　　　　　　—Elbert Hubbard

The information industry now accounts for 60 percent of the work force. There are over 100 million computers, word processors, and terminals on desks in offices worldwide. You can have your computer programmed with everything from a dictionary to a database management system. But you can't get one equipped with intuition. Computers cannot make value judgments. They can't express opinions or speculate. Only you can do all those things. Your judgment is the most important element in the management equation.

Reflections:

As a manager, you must be adept at analytical thinking. But, you must also have the strong interpersonal skills to relate to, motivate, and lead others. You have to keep in touch with your staff and set an open-door policy. Do your staff members call you by your first name? Do they invite you to lunch? Can you count on them, as friends, to keep you well informed? Does the relationship go beyond the office? It's not enough to "know the numbers," you have to know your co-workers.

I have to count on more than my computer. I have to count on people.

*"The real danger is not that computers
will begin to think like men, but that
men will begin to think like computers."*
—Sidney J. Harris

The number of industrial robots in the United States rose from only 3,000 in 1979 to a projected 150,000 units today. The pioneer of robotics, Norbert Weiner, feared that people might become like cybers. (The word *cyber* is classical Greek for "steersman," an allusion to a machine's ability to react to feedback and adjust course.) Our brain and nervous system control our operations through feedback, too. We learn from mistakes, and our jerky, faltering movements become smooth and coordinated because our subconscious has stored the myriad steps to the goal. But, unlike machines, we can control our thoughts.

Reflections:

When you start to approach your work in a rote manner, without questioning your actions and without looking for new ways to work, you become efficient, not necessarily effective. The challenge is to look beyond your short-term goal to a larger, overarching goal: which is not just efficiency, but effectiveness.

Effectiveness lies in doing less in order to do better.

"An egotist is not one who thinks so much of himself as so little of others."
—Herman L. Wayland

In all our dealings, we strive to interpret events in a way that is to our advantage. For example, when working on a team project, we're apt to stress the importance of our own role and minimize the contributions of others. We may take a disproportionate share of the credit and avoid all blame. Or, as one pundit put it, "An honest executive is one who shares the credit with the man who did all the work."

Reflections:

A tightly knit team consistently outperforms a group of individuals. Members of a team work together toward a common goal; instead of competing with each other, they compete with other companies. But subordinating your self-interest to that of the team's is not easy. The natural tendency is to look out for number one. To guard against this behavior, suspend judgment when working in a brainstorming session. Listen attentively, show enthusiasm for the ideas of others; hitchhike on their ideas; and encourage others to do the same.

I'm going to make an extra effort to give credit where it's due.

"Research is to see what everybody has seen, and to think what nobody else has thought."
—Albert Szent-Györgyi

Albert Szent-Györgyi, who won the Nobel Prize for discovering vitamin C and its function, and who also did pioneering work on biochemistry, could not, or would not, write a grant proposal! He said that he didn't know how to express his ideas or describe his anticipated results. If he could put his ideas in writing, he didn't think the experiment was worth doing. Could someone like Szent-Györgyi work for you? Would you be able to see past his or her eccentricities and focus on the strengths?

Reflections:

Effective managers focus on their subordinates' strengths and assign them projects that they can succeed at. Rather than becoming hypercritical about blind spots, these managers encourage excellence through constant genuine praise. The more people sense what you expect of them, the higher their personal standards become. How often do you praise each member of your staff?

There is no such thing as a passing remark when it includes a compliment.

*"Criticism comes easier than craftsman-
ship."*

—Zeuxis

One way of dealing with our problems and fears
is to project them onto others. Projection puts some
distance between us and the problem and makes it
easier to manage our feelings because we seem
blameless. But in order for projection to work, we
need a scapegoat, someone to criticize when things
go wrong. When we refuse to accept responsibility
for our own problems and blame others, the original
problem is compounded by the feeling that we are
being victimized by the person we blame.

Reflections:

Workaholics live in fear of being victimized, yet
we put ourselves in that position every time we
blame someone else for our problems. If you feel put
upon, it's legitimate to ask why you allow the situation to continue. What are you getting out of it?
What fears and problems might you possibly be
projecting onto someone else?

*Before criticizing someone else, I will examine my-
self.*

"Too often we ... enjoy the comfort of opinion without the discomfort of thought."

—John F. Kennedy

A trade association was roasting a member, and his partner took to the podium. "You and I have been through a lot together, Phil," the partner said. "During that wildcat strike, you were there by my side. And when fire nearly destroyed our business, you were there. Yes, when sales slumped, inventories backed up, and we had to let 10 percent of our staff go, you were always right there. No matter what went wrong, Phil, you were there every time. You know, it's finally dawned on me, Phil," he said, "You're bad luck!"

Reflections:

Of course, the business partner was joking. But many of us do have a Phil in our company—someone we blame no matter what goes wrong. One way of relieving tension is by blaming someone else for all our troubles. It's easier to blame that person than ourselves. You know you're projecting your own feelings onto someone else when you catch yourself generalizing ("Isn't that just like him! He always screws up a job"). When that happens, ask yourself, "What are you really afraid to face?"

Instead of pointing a finger, I'll lend a hand.

"If you are a perfectionist, you are guaranteed to be a loser in everything you do."

—David Burns, M.D.

Success is not perfection; success is being slightly above average. For example, Thomas Edison succeeded despite numerous setbacks and failures. Only thirteen of the 1,069 patents he obtained resulted in fundamentally new products that were successful in the marketplace. In other words, he truly succeeded only 1.2 percent of the time. Only when we admit our mistakes can we learn from them and grow. When was the last time you admitted you were wrong?

Reflections:

Workaholics set such high standards that nothing short of perfection satisfies us. But perfection is an illusion; everything in life can be improved if we try hard enough. The result is that we workaholics are never satisfied with our own performance, nor that of our co-workers. We live with a sense of constant frustration and failure, the gnawing feeling that we should be doing more. And, for lack of a better idea, we criticize.

The biggest mistake I can make is to ignore the fact that I'm in the wrong.

*"A problem well stated is a problem half
solved."*
—Charles F. Kettering

Charles Kettering was second only to Thomas
Edison in the number of major inventions he pat-
ented. The father of the self-starting engine and
high-octane gas, he didn't have much regard for the
"slide rule boys," the so-called experts whose
knowledge clouded their vision of what was possible. He believed in the power of "intelligent ignorance" and assigned major projects to people
unschooled in the subjects, whose thinking wasn't
influenced by preconceived notions about the problem.

Reflections:

We workaholics pride ourselves on our knowledge of our businesses. We try to impress others by
having all the answers. But Charles Kettering looked
for people who had more questions than answers.
He knew that breakthroughs are often made against
all odds by the naive, inspired amateur with a completely open mind, who stumbles on an idea because he or she didn't know it "couldn't be done."
Are you nurturing the young talent in your firm by
sharing your knowledge in a way that isn't intimi-
dating?

*I'm going to take the time to work closely with the
younger people on the staff.*

"Failure is only the opportunity to more intelligently begin anew."
—Henry Ford

When Henry Ford visited his parents' birthplace—Dublin, Ireland—the dignitaries feted him at an extravagant banquet. Afterward, they asked for a donation to a hospital fund drive, to which Ford promptly donated $5,000. However, the next day's headlines read, "Ford Donates $50,000." His hosts offered to print a retraction, "Ford Only Donates $5,000", but Henry saw things differently. "I'll donate the full $50,000," he said, "if I can choose the inscription over the hospital door." And so the hospital got its donation, and Ford got the last word, for over the door it reads, "I was a stranger, and you took me in."

Reflections:

Workaholics always want to have the last word. We have an answer for everything. Unlike Henry Ford, we have trouble laughing at ourselves when someone gets the best of us. In order to protect our self-esteem, we may refuse to admit we're wrong, rationalize our position, and repeat the same mistake over and over again. The next time someone gets the best of you in a discussion, laugh it off. As Doctor Lawrence Peter, author of *The Peter Principle*, says, "If you don't learn from your mistakes, there's no sense making them."

The next time I make a mistake, I'm going to laugh it off.

JULY 18

"Men are not against you; they are mere-ly for themselves."

—Gene Fowler

It could be a sales prospect who slams the phone down in your ear, or a vendor who bills you for more than the original quote. It could be a client who cancels an order in mid-project, or an employee who refuses to work overtime. Whatever the incident, your critical spirit is quick to find fault. The object of your ire may be the person who didn't treat you "fairly," but the root cause of your anger is a misguided idea of what fairness means. Fairness is an abstract, subjective concept that depends on your point of view.

Reflections:

Each of us sees things differently. The prospect who hung up on you may have been expecting an important call. The vendor who billed more than he or she quoted may not have included sales tax in that bid. The client who canceled the project may be short on funds. And the employee who didn't work overtime may have another commitment. What's fair to one may not appear fair to another. You can't control how other people view reality. So why make yourself angry by being so critical?

When I try to exercise too much control, I'm not being fair to myself.

JULY 19

"Pay no attention to what the critics say; no statue has ever been put up to a critic."

—Jean Sibelius

Job stress is contagious. It breeds in situations where there is role ambiguity, interpersonal conflict, politics, rigid regulation, excess work loads, dull repetitive work, and a lack of incentives. It's spread by co-workers who are cynical, critical malcontents, the kind of people who brighten up a room by leaving it. No one would accuse them of being workaholics, but they sure are carriers because their attitude makes your job harder.

Reflections:

There's no such thing as a perfect working atmosphere. Every company has its share of problems. But finding fault, as some people do, simply undermines morale. When an isolated problem occurs, they overgeneralize and see it as part of a bigger pattern. ("No one *ever* tells us what's going on around here.") When in doubt, they jump to a negative conclusion. ("There's no way that the client will approve this plan.") And when things go right, they discount the news. ("Swell, we got that big contract—now we have to work overtime.") They simply can't see the positive side of anything. If you want to lower your stress level, avoid malcontents.

I need friends who put the stress on positive thinking.

"Imagination is a poor substitute for experience."

—Havelock Ellis

How many times have you made a phone call only to hear the other person say, "I was just about to call you." Or, spoken up in a meeting to have someone else say, "You took the words right out of my mouth." Coincidences like that happen often enough that it's easy to fall into the trap of "mind reading," especially when you work closely with someone. You think you know them so well that you assign attitudes and motives to them without finding out how they actually feel. If they don't react the way you expect, you become upset and the other person is left wondering why.

Reflections:

You know you're mind reading when you start attributing attitudes and motives to people, labeling them in your mind as "good" or "bad," and using highly emotional language to describe their behavior. If someone's behavior surprises you, speak to them in private about what's bothering you. You might be surprised to learn what's really on his or her mind.

Before criticizing someone, I will check out my facts.

"Most men when they think they are thinking are merely rearranging their prejudices."

—Knute Rockne

In the intensely competitive world of the workaholic, you're either one of "us" or one of "them." When an employee quits to join a competitor, he or she instantly becomes one of "them," the enemy, a pariah. Despite years of loyal, dedicated service to the company, he or she is now seen as a turncoat. Without minimizing the importance of trade secrets and confidentiality, it must be said that most such characterizations do the ex-employee and the company a disservice.

Reflections:

Any time someone resigns, you owe it to yourself to find out why he or she is leaving. At the same time, you want to observe business protocol with respect to the actual departure. A valued employee, who leaves on good terms, may someday be an ambassador of goodwill for the company; and might even return, bringing new skills to the job—providing you don't slam the door behind him or her.

I'm going to stay on good terms with my former associates.

"I am still learning."
                    —Michelangelo's motto

Of the forty-four statues Michelangelo sculpted, only fourteen were completed. The others were abandoned when the master's mallet and chisel uncovered some hidden flaw in the marble. All of us have hidden flaws that are revealed under the stress and strain of business. When you hire someone, you don't really know what that person is made of for about six months. No matter how good you think such recruits are, some will crack and crumble, and there is nothing you can do about it but learn from the experience.

Reflections:

People are not cold, lifeless blocks of marble to be discarded because they don't measure up to your standards. If someone isn't meeting your expectations, discuss the problem in a way that preserves his or her dignity. Hold the discussion in private, be specific in describing your concerns, and state the steps you expect the person to take. Make sure your bench marks are measurable and meaningful and that they fall within the job description. Finally, set a date for reviewing progress. If the person is unable to satisfy your concerns, rather than chip away at self-esteem, help him or her find another job.

If someone I hired isn't succeeding, I share some of the responsibility.

JULY 23

*"Treat your friends as you do your pic-
tures and place them in the best light."*
—Jennie Jerome Churchill

Most of us have no trouble seeing flaws in others that we overlook in ourselves. When we point
out their shortcomings, it's always for "their own
good" and the good of the company. But if our criticism isn't delivered tactfully, it can threaten self-
esteem, undermine confidence, and kill morale. Instead of improving their performance, our criticism
may worsen it.

Reflections:

Before criticizing someone, make sure you get
your facts straight. Try to identify the cause of the
problem and the person responsible. It makes no
sense to blame everyone, because that simply weakens morale. Once you have all the facts, speak to the
responsible person in private, without losing your
temper. Listen to what he or she says, and make
clear how you feel. Be specific about the improve-
ments you expect, make a record of the conversation, and then forget it.

*In criticizing someone else's work, I'll treat him or
her as I would want to be treated.*

"Nothing is so easy as to deceive one's self."

—Demosthenes

You know you're feeling superior when you start referring to yourself in the third person, call your memos *documents*, and have your secretary place your outgoing phone calls for you. A sense of superiority makes it difficult to learn from others because it lulls us into thinking that we're somehow different and incapable of making the same errors that others make.

Reflections:

Bishop Fulton Sheen said, "Self-knowledge demands the discovery of our predominant fault," which is difficult to do if you think you're incapable of grave error. To discover your predominant fault, ask yourself, "What do I think about most when I'm alone? Where do my thoughts go spontaneously?" For many workaholics, the answer lies in fantasies of success, power, and prestige. We are so caught up in our ambitions that we fail to see our own limitations. Truly successful executives have a realistic view of their own human frailties. As a result, they not only learn from their own mistakes but those of others as well.

It's important to not feel self-important.

"A man never discloses his own character so clearly as when he describes another's."

—Jean Paul Richter

In 1941, the art collection of William Randolph Hearst was among the world's largest. But the media magnate had to sell his artwork to offset huge losses in his newspaper empire. When Hearst learned that the gallery commissioned to sell his masterpieces had decided to hold the auction at Gimbel's department store, he was apoplectic at the idea of his artwork being acquired by "subway trade." As a compromise, the gallery agreed to also hold the auction at the more prestigious Sak's Fifth Avenue. To Hearst's amazement, Gimbel's far outsold Sak's.

Reflections:

Hearst made the same mistake so many of us make when we label people as "lazy," "SOBs," or "lightweights." Stereotyped critical thinking is common among workaholics because it is a form of mental shorthand or snap judgment. But when we caricature someone and oversimplify, we are setting ourselves up for a surprise. At the same time, we are apt to earn his or her enmity—and just possibly, a label of our own.

Since I don't like to be labeled, I shouldn't label others.

JULY 26

"Honesty is often in the wrong."
—Lucan

The ancient Egyptians worshiped Maat, the goddess of scales, who measured the precise weight of each soul by using a feather as a counterbalance. Many of us are just as precise in measuring and weighing every person with whom we come in contact. We take their slightest fault into account, and we are quick to share our "frank and honest opinion." But while honesty is the best policy, it is not necessarily the best practice. More often than not, constructive criticism is destructive, and we are better off keeping our honest opinions to ourselves.

Reflections:

Could you be more lenient and less judgmental in your dealings with others? No one is perfect, and you're sure to be disappointed if you don't allow others a margin of error in their dealings with you. Guard against critical thoughts, no matter how honest they may seem because they sow doubt and confusion. As Abraham Lincoln said, "tact is the ability to describe others as they see themselves."

There's more to being honest than telling the truth.

"Only a mediocre person is always at his best."

—W. Somerset Maugham

When Alexander the Great defeated Egypt, he had himself declared pharaoh, a position that went beyond kingship to that of a deity. Thereafter he spoke of himself as a god, which did not sit well with his historian, Callisthenes, who thought that Alexander's fame and glory were a product of his (Callisthenes') pen. Callisthenes was too close to Alexander, too familiar with his human foibles, to write about him as a god. At the same time, Alexander was uncomfortable under the critical gaze of his publicist. He had Callisthenes put to death.

Reflections:

Alexander's narcissism is an extreme example of our need to see ourselves as superior. We workaholics have a tendency to treat subordinates as rivals and to compete with them for honors and accolades. The danger is that we will surround ourselves with sycophants who tell us what we want to hear, rather than what we need to hear. Adlai Stevenson put the matter in its proper perspective when he said, "Flattery is all right—if you don't inhale."

In order to succeed, I have to promote my co-workers.

"Your verdict on others will be the verdict passed on you."
—Matthew 7:2

When you smile, you use seventeen facial muscles, but when you frown, you use forty-three. Being hard-nosed is hard work! All that frowning, grumbling, and complaining about the work of others can take a lot out of you. If you've become bitter and critical, the easiest way to change your attitude is to change your behavior. Start smiling, even when you don't feel like it, and your disposition will become sunnier. It's a psychological fact that a change in behavior leads to a change in personality.

Reflections:
Accepting others as they are is a gift we give ourselves because it frees us of negative, destructive thoughts and emotions. If you find yourself dwelling on the shortcomings of others, you need only recall when you did something similar to understand how the other person feels about the mistake. The quicker way to smooth out the wrinkles in a relationship is with a smile.

My attitude is only as sunny as my smile.

JULY 29

"The bow too tensely strung is easily broken."

—Publilius Syrus

When you talk to yourself, what tone of voice do you use? Does your inner voice sound stern, authoritarian, and highly critical? Do you tell yourself you "should" work through lunch hour, you "must" put in overtime, and you "ought" to work this weekend? Such statements are attempts at taut self-control that pull you apart between feeling exhausted and feeling guilty. Under the constant strain, you can snap like a violin string that isn't loosened between performances.

Reflections:

There are times when you have to work overtime, and it is important to know when they occur so you can prepare mentally for them. Yet your thought patterns can become automatic, and you can slip into thinking you "should" or "must" work overtime when it isn't necessary. To guard against this tendency, you need a coping strategy. Before working overtime, ask yourself, "Why should I? Who says it's necessary? Am I overreacting?" Learn to take time off without feeling guilty.

From now on, I'm going to give myself credit for a job well done whenever I handle a project without working overtime.

JULY 30

"If the critics were always right we should be in deep trouble."
—Robert Morley

Management is not a popularity contest. If you are overly sensitive to criticism and hesitate to make unpopular decisions because of what others might think, you're not doing your job. Whether it's determining vacation schedules or deciding who answers the phones at lunch hour, choosing a health care vendor or deciding the bonus pool formula—whatever the issue, you're not going to please everyone, so don't try.

Reflections:

Criticism by others is often an affirmation that you're thinking for yourself. It's unrealistic to expect others to think as you do on every subject; after all, their perception of reality differs from yours. Neither of you is necessarily right, but you're the one getting paid to decide. Instead of being upset with your detractors and attacking them in true workaholic fashion, lighten up. They're not criticizing you. They're criticizing your actions. You're not responsible for their feelings; only they can control how they feel; and they'll probably come around to your way of thinking, if they see your ideas work.

If I try to please everyone, I'll please no one.

JULY 31

"Only great men have great faults."
                              —French proverb

During the Civil War, President Lincoln decided to appoint Ulysses S. Grant as general of all the Union troops on the strength of his outstanding record in the field of battle. But when word of his pending decision reached several congressmen, who knew Grant to be a heavy drinker, they reproached Lincoln, saying, "The man is a drunkard!" "Yes," answered Lincoln, thoughtfully, "and when I find out what brand of whiskey he drinks, I intend to send a case to all our generals."

Reflections:
If Lincoln had been a skeptical, acerbic workaholic, looking for fault, he certainly would have found it in General Grant. But, the president focused on performance, not personality. He knew that despite his drinking Grant was a superb field commander. Lincoln overlooked the general's shortcomings and brought out his strengths, the way a good manager should. Many great people have great faults, or, as personnel consultant Paul Goodman said, "Few great men could pass Personnel." In dealing with your subordinates, focus on their strengths, instead of their weaknesses.

My strength as a manager depends on my ability to develop the strengths of others.

AUGUST

Keeping Score

As a result of our competitiveness, we are obsessed with keeping score. We quantify everything to find out who's winning and losing. The one thing we never count is the number of times our workaholic behavior has diminished the quality of our lives and our relationships. We need to make a list of people to whom we should make amends, starting with ourselves.

AUGUST 1

"The happiest people seem to be those who have no particular reason for being happy except that they are so."
—W. R. Inge

The term *statistics* was coined by Sir John Sinclair in 1791, when he wrote *A Statistical Account of Scotland*. In the preface to his book, Sinclair said his purpose was to measure "the quantum of happiness enjoyed by the inhabitants and the means of improvement." Ever since, we have been trying to reduce our "happiness quotient" to a single number, the bigger the better. The closest we have ever been able to come is a number aptly described as our "gross income."

Reflections:

Grandiosity can lead us to set unrealistic financial goals and depreciate the small gains along the way. It's as if we're constantly saying to ourselves, "You think this is good? This is nothing! Wait and see." Instead of forestalling your happiness, celebrate the minor victories with small prizes for yourself—silly, inexpensive, inconsequential prizes that are of no value to anyone but you (otherwise they become points in a competitive game).

Today I'm going to give myself credit for the minor victories along the way.

AUGUST 2

*"Why does a slight tax increase cost you
two hundred dollars and a substantial
tax cut save you twenty cents?"*
—Peg Bracken

If money is the way we keep score in the game
of life, the scorekeeper must be the Internal Revenue
Service. Unfortunately, the IRS changes the rules of
the game so often, it's hard to tell what your after-
tax earnings are. Before 1976, major changes in the
tax codes occurred every six to eight years, but now
there are major changes annually. In one year alone,
there were forty eight completely new tax forms,
over a hundred other forms were revised, and the
IRS manual totaled over 40,000 pages. The boggle
factor is so high that the IRS toll-free hotline has a
30.8 percent error rate.

Reflections:

Someone once said, "Only two things in life are
certain—death and taxes." Today, you can't even be
certain of taxes. Those firm, hard numbers that
added up to a tax break a few years ago have been
erased by hundreds of IRS regulations, private letter
rulings, published rulings, and court cases. All
backed by 154 different penalties. Do you really
want your self-worth linked to such an arbitrary,
changeable standard as Line 30 of Form 1040?

*One thing I'm certain of: my true worth can't be
measured in dollars and cents.*

*"The trouble with today's economy is
that when a man is rich, it's all on paper. When he's broke, it's cash."*
— Sam Marconi

It might seem sensible for a company to keep its
books in a consistent manner from year to year, but
logic doesn't always prevail over "generally accepted accounting procedures." Since inception, the Financial Accounting Standards Board has advocated
changes in the reporting of everything from R&D ex-
penses, inventory, leases, and depreciation to employee benefits and pension fund liabilities. With
one small change in a footnote, set in six-point type,
yesterday's paper profits become today's cash losses.

Reflections:

Business is not a science. The laws of accounting are subject to change and your numbers are always open to question. If your emotional balance
and your balance sheet are one and the same, you
can expect a setback sooner or later. But if you're
able to separate your ego from the business, and analyze the numbers objectively, you stand a better
chance of realizing more than paper profits.

*I'm going to work the numbers instead of having the
numbers work me.*

AUGUST 4

"You can name the price if I can name the terms."
                              —Mishulam Riklis

To the natives of the Maldive Islands, the medium of exchange was Cowrie shells; to the Inuit of Hudson Bay it was walrus tusks; at various other times and places the standards of value have been fish hooks, coffee beans, feathers and cigarettes. In truth, the marketplace has no enduring standard of value. What we prize today we trivialize tomorrow. At one time, the U.S. dollar could be exchanged for gold; now it is backed by the "full faith and credit of the U.S. government," whatever those terms mean.

Reflections:

Bond swaps, option straddles, commodity futures: They sure sound more sophisticated than Cowrie shells. But the truth is they, too, are storehouses of questionable value. In fact, if you were to examine your entire investment portfolio, tally all your bank accounts and calculate the worth of all your real estate, they would be nothing when compared to the truly worthwhile things in life. There is no denomination large enough to express such values as love, truth, honor, and peace of mind. They are available in unlimited supply to all who seek them.

The things of lasting value are priceless.

"Anyone who thinks there is safety in numbers hasn't looked at the stock market pages."

—Irene Peters

The situation in the financial markets is so topsy-turvy that the newest form of one-up-manship is fighting for the bragging rights about your club's biggest portfolio loss. It's not a question of who made more money, but who took the bigger hit in a REIT, oil and gas partnership, railroad tank car, cattle, or other so-called tax shelter. The fact is most of us are working too hard to make our money work hard for us, or, as one disgruntled investor put it, "Out of sight, out of mind means out of pocket, too."

Reflections:

Get-rich-quick schemes have a seductive appeal to workaholics who expect their money to work as hard as they do. But most of us are too busy managing our careers to figure out what's really going on in markets where good news is greeted as bad and bad news is trumpeted as good. An upturn in employment is seen as inflationary, but a drop in retail sales is good for an overheating economy. An orgy of mergers sends the market into paroxysms of delight, and a drop in interest rates buoys the bond market. If nothing seems to add up any more, maybe it never did.

One of the best investments I can make is a contribution to a local charity.

AUGUST 6

"Happiness is positive cash flow."
— Fred Adler

What do you do when the numbers don't go according to plan, when all those spreadsheets don't add up to your minimum daily adult requirement of peace of mind? Do you work longer hours again? Do you say, "I shoulda . . ."; "I have to . . ."; "I must . . ."? Do you make excuses, blame bad luck, and engage in wishful thinking ("If only . . .")? It's one thing to be a recovering workaholic when your business is sound; it's quite another thing to be one when your bottom line is heading south.

Reflections:

Just when you have your life in order and your work in perspective, your business disrupts your peace of mind. The problems are real enough, you're not imagining them, they're sitting right on top of your desk. That's what makes this situation so threatening to your recovery. At the first sign of real trouble, your workaholic conscience says, "This never would have happened if you'd worked harder." If you're not careful, you can talk yourself into a relapse. Yes, there are times when overtime is necessary, but set a limit, keep track of your hours, and reward yourself for the extra effort.

If I don't set my limits, others will gladly set them for me.

"There are two ways to get enough: one is to accumulate more and more, the other is to desire less."

—G. K. Chesterton

Many of us equate our net worth with our self-worth in a habit of thought entrained in us from childhood. In school, we measured ourselves by the grades we earned. Later, we learned to keep score by the size of our "gross income" and perks: the stock options and insurance plans; the company car and special parking stall; the country club and condominium. The net result can be a diminished sense of self-worth. Billionaire Bunker T. Hunt must have sensed something like that when he said, "If you know how much you're worth, you're probably not worth much." Shortly afterward, Hunt lost much of his fortune in a reckless attempt to corner the world silver market.

Reflections:

How much are you worth? The answer cannot be arrived at with a calculator. Your true worth is beyond measure. In the eyes of your Higher Power, you are priceless. There has never been, nor is there now, nor will there ever be, anyone in the history of this universe quite like you. You are unique. More precious than all the world's silver, there is only one you.

My true worth does not depend on how much I take home, but on what I give back.

AUGUST 8

"Quantity has a quality all its own."
—Nikolai Lenin

We workaholics count everything. Money. Perks. Possessions. We keep score in order to find out who's winning in the game of life; in so doing, we reduce the quality of our life to the lowest common denominator. With the advent of computers and electronic spreadsheets, we no longer labor over rows and columns of figures: we simply ask, "What if .... " punch a few keys, and watch. The figures dance across the screen, and suddenly, it becomes crystal clear that the answers only make sense if we ask the right questions—like, why are we working so hard? How much is enough? And, why bother counting?

Reflections:

Ultimately, all counting is a form of long division—dividing everything into two piles, mine and yours. The very act of counting, weighing, and measuring in order to place a value on something is aggressive. We need to accept the fact that our self-worth does not depend on how much wealth, power, and prestige we acquire. When we can contemplate and appreciate things without possessing them, there will be no limits to our happiness.

I don't have to calculate to appreciate.

AUGUST 9

*"There is no way of keeping profits up
by keeping wages down."*
—David Ricardo

The original fast track to success was the Via Salaria, or Salt Road, one of the most heavily traveled routes to Imperial Rome. Roman soldiers received part of their pay in salt, known as *salarium argentum*, from which we derive the word "salary." If a soldier was promoted and his pay increased, it was said that he was "worth his salt," an expression we still use today. Determining someone's value to the company and rewarding him or her is one of the most difficult challenges a manager faces.

Reflections:

As a workaholic manager, you may be tempted to set unrealistic goals or withhold rewards for some inconsequential reason. By the time you distribute the awards, they've lost their value. Money, like salt, is useless once it goes stale. Be generous in rewarding those who work for you or they may conclude that the fast track leads to a salt mine.

In rewarding my staff, I reward myself in the long run.

"The bigger the bankroll, the tighter the rubber band."

—Anonymous

We tend to think of our possessions as extensions of ourselves. As we acquire more and more things, the limits of the self are stretched to the breaking point like a rubber band around a bankroll. The more we take into our lives, the more uptight we become. Every threat to our possessions becomes a threat to us, and we try to defend ourselves on every side. The very things we look to for security and serenity create fear and anxiety as they tarnish, rust, fade, and fall apart.

Reflections:

Constantly stretching ourselves to the limit creates so much stress and strain that we lose our elasticity and our ability to snap back in a real crisis. We have to be willing to relax and let go. But that is extremely difficult so long as we measure our self-worth according to our possessions. The truly successful person knows how to enjoy things without getting all wound up over who owns them.

The best things in life are free.

> *"The only problems money can solve are money problems."*
>
> —Laurence J. Peter

Legend has it that an Indian scholar named Sessa invented chess and that the maharajah was so delighted he offered the scholar any reward he wanted. The wily Sessa asked for as many grains of wheat as it would take to cover the chessboard, if each square had double the grains of the preceding square. The maharajah ordered his lackeys to fulfill the request, but later learned, to his chagrin, that the count would total 18,446,744,073,709,551,615 grains! Not to be outwitted, he insisted that Sessa count each grain himself—an impossible task.

Reflections:

Sessa's fate was the same as that of anyone whose overreaching ambition leads to an endless counting of riches. The process is all consuming. As long as we persist in keeping score, we can't possibly win. Overflowing riches invariably foster the idea that money itself must be made to work. In the end, the wealthy must constantly work at employing their money—their Midas touch becomes a crushing grip. They can never stop keeping score.

My goals should be just beyond reach, but within my grasp.

"If you make money your god, it will plague you like the devil."
—Henry Fielding

If you plotted on a graph an executive's lifetime earnings, they would follow a bell-shaped curve, peaking around age forty five and gradually declining. The raises come less often; the bonuses shrink; the promotions go to someone else. Eventually, we find ourselves working harder than ever for a "kid" ten years our junior who doesn't know "half of what we've forgotten." This is tough stuff for a workaholic to handle. We're accustomed to winning! Of course, there are exceptions—friends whose careers continue their upward trajectory—but that only adds to our frustration. If they can do it, why can't we?

Reflections:

Remember when you loved your work? Your paycheck was a bonus twice a month! It isn't until we reach the limits of our ability and earning power that we feel the true emptiness of a work-centered life. When others pass us by, we begin to question why we're in the race. If it's only for the money, we're sure to lose. The true winner, Emerson said, is the one who recognizes, "The reward of a thing well done, is to have done it."

As long as my spiritual income exceeds my spiritual outgo, I'm successful.

"Success is not as greedy as people think, but insignificant. That's why it satisfies nobody."

—Seneca

One major stressor in everyone's life is finances: we never seem to have enough money to satisfy all our desires. Society encourages us to "Live for the moment," "Enjoy it while it lasts," "Buy now, pay later." If your family is typical, you owe 16 cents of debt for every dollar of income; and that's on top of a crushing mortgage payment. Never in our history have families shouldered such a debt load. At the same time, the savings rate has dropped to 4 percent of disposable income. Most of us simply do not have enough savings to weather a financial crisis. The result is low-level chronic stress.

Reflections:

The accumulation of wealth is one way in which workaholics keep score. But since other people don't know how much we make, our income is soon converted to status symbols such as an exotic car and big home. We mortgage our peace of mind and pay for our anxiety on the installment plan. So long as we count our wealth in dollars and cents, we'll never have enough to pay off the debt. At some point, we have to put a price on our serenity. How much have you built up in your spiritual bank account?

I need to develop an attitude of gratitude.

AUGUST 14

"If it can't be measured, it can't be managed."

—Ken Blanchard

We live in a world of uncertainty, where hard facts and figures are a scarce and valuable resource in the hands of someone who knows how to use them. No doubt you have a strong bias toward facts and figures, or you wouldn't be a workaholic. But your fascination with numbers can leave you swimming in a sea of data far from the shoreline of knowledge.

Reflections:

To avoid getting lost in the numbers, you need a set of norms or key business ratios to help you organize the data. Start by asking yourself, "What do I need to know, and what measurements will help?" If numbers are not available for all calculations, make an informed guess. Before actually doing the calculations, estimate the answer, and if the actual total surprises you, rethink the formula. Write out each step in the operation so you can backtrack. Round all numbers to two digits so they're easier to work with. It's also easier to compare numbers when reading down rather than across the page. Keep in mind, numbers are only meaningful when compared to something else.

My grasp of the business is only as good as my grasp of the numbers.

"You can't sit there dead in the water. You have to do whatever necessary to solve the problem—right now. You have to decide."

—Thomas Watson, Jr.

Most business decisions would be simple if the only thing to consider were the numbers, but that only happens in the business school case studies. In the real world, numbers do not tell the whole story. There are subjective, unquantifiable values to be weighed, as well; and if the situation calls for an unpopular decision, our emotions may distort the numbers. The logical left brain urges us to act, while the intuitive right brain accuses us of being driven by numbers. Should we be objective or subjective? Can we make up the rules as we go along?

Reflections:

Numbers only appear to be objective. They are actually subjective values in that we decide what to measure and how. The closest we come to an objective standard is the bottom line. Basing decisions on how they affect the bottom line may not seem fair (whatever that is), but it is consistent with the long-term interests of everyone in business. The moment we ignore the bottom line in favor of a more subjective approach, we complicate things.

The simplest solution is one tied to the bottom line.

AUGUST 16

"A conclusion is the place where you grew tired of thinking."

—Martin Fischer

Numbers have crisp, sharp edges. A problem that can be reduced to a number is somehow neater and tidier; better yet, it can be expressed in a formula, so the results are repeatable. That's why workaholics like numbers: they're so orderly, so predictable. In problem solving, we try to reduce everything to a number, preferably one carried to three decimal points, no rounding off. We'd rather be precisely wrong than vaguely right.

Reflections:

Despite their apparent precision, many numbers are irrational. Consider the mathematical symbol pi, which stands for an irrational number whose digits march randomly toward infinity. (For convenience sake, it is usually abbreviated as 3.14159.) At one point in the extended string of numbers, a pattern seems to appear: seven 3's in a row. Since the odds against such a run are about 10 million to one, it might seem like more than a chance occurrence. But the fact is, if you search for *any* sort of unusual seven-digit pattern, the odds of finding one go way up. Put differently, if you run enough numbers in search of any pattern, eventually you'll come to the wrong conclusion.

Numbers seldom hold the entire answer.

"For every problem there is a solution and usually the best solution is the nearest at hand."

—David Mahoney

"Wrestling with the numbers" is something every workaholic does when we don't like the answer the computer supplies. The figures may suggest dropping a product line, canceling a project, or firing a friend. Whatever the solution, we fight it and grapple with the numbers, trying to get a hold on the problem, a hold that could twist things to our advantage. But numbers are obstinate things. We can't bend them to our will.

Reflections:

If you find yourself tumbling the numbers over and over again in your mind, you're probably wrestling with the obvious. In your gut, you know what to do. The best solution is the simplest, and every other solution complicates your life so that you have to work harder. Ask yourself what you are avoiding. Is it really as bad as what you're putting yourself through now, or what you might put yourself through by acting on what you know? Maybe it's time to stop running the numbers and start running your business again.

The longer I wait to act, the worse the numbers become.

"Do not put your faith in what statistics say until you have carefully considered what they do not say."
—William W. Watt

We all want to be above average at our jobs. But *average* is a slippery term. It can mean the median, mean, or mode, and in each case the value may change. To get the mean, you divide the total by the number of individuals. To get the median, you find the midpoint between the upper and lower halves. And to get the mode, you look for the individuals that occur most often. There is no such thing as a "true average," so all such comparisons are misleading.

Reflections:

By "average," most of us mean the people we compare ourselves to at work. They become our "mode," however misrepresentative the group might be. For example, you may be at the top of your profession, earning far more than the median or mean, but if your co-workers (your "mode") earn more, you feel below average. Yet you may earn more than your co-workers, and earn less than the mean or median, in which case you still feel below average. What difference does it really make, anyway?

I'm above average as long as I don't compare myself to the average.

> *"As far as the laws of mathematics refer to reality, they are not certain, and as far as they are certain, they do not refer to reality."*
>
> —Albert Einstein

According to the quantum mechanical view of reality, matter results from the chance encounter of numberless subatomic particles. Galaxies, stars, planets, and asteroids; mountains, seas, insects, fish, and animals; all are said to be different faces on the same die, tumbled together for eons to form new combinations and permutations. It's a universe, physicists say, in which the creative power of numbers is beyond question. But is it?

Reflections:

You can run the numbers as long as you like, and they will not add up to one creative idea. Numbers, per se, have no meaning. They are merely symbols to which you attach meaning; and in so doing, you create a new order. For example, you may say sales are up 5 percent; your boss may say they're down compared to last year; and your assistant might point out that you're gaining on the competition. You're all viewing the same numbers from a different vantage point. In that sense, you create your own quantum mechanical reality.

I'm going to focus on the positive aspects of reality.

"Chance favors the prepared mind."
—Louis Pasteur

The more successful we become, the less likely we are to attribute our good fortune to luck. We say things like "The harder I work, the luckier I get. . . . ," "I make my own breaks. . . . ," and "I get lucky after a fourteen-hour day." By placing so much emphasis on work, those simplistic catchphrases gloss over the fact that good fortune is usually the result of the complex interaction of nature, nurture, and chance. You're left thinking if you work hard enough at anything, you can get lucky. However, it's just not that simple.

Reflections:

Yes, hard work is essential for success. But it also helps to have the good fortune to be born in a nation with a high standard of living, a free enterprise system, and expanding economy. It helps to have nurturing parents, access to a free education, and the native ability to compete effectively in the job market. Finally, it helps to be blessed with talent and a temperament that attracts supporters and enables you to take risks and recover from setbacks that might overwhelm others. When you add up the score, be sure to count those lucky breaks.

Luck is a matter of chance. What I do with it is a matter of choice.

"We never reduced the art of management to a formula. We could never be sure we were right on any one specific decision."

—Harold Geneen

Under Harold Geneen, ITT was a money-making machine, posting increased earnings for fifty-eight consecutive quarters, a record in the annals of U.S. industry. Geneen believed in taking a "calculated risk." But, he also knew that most risks cannot be calculated with a high degree of probability—there is always a rogue factor that distorts our projections.

Reflections:

Most of us are adept at calculating our risks and rewards, but we have difficulty calculating the odds; probabilistic thinking doesn't come naturally. That's why a prudent executive takes a flexible approach to planning, using the numbers as a general guide only. If you rely solely on the numbers, you may overlook some key environmental information. Numbers are abstractions, and as such they leave something out. Why not get out from behind your spreadsheets and meet with your customers and vendors for a day?

A flexible approach to planning can improve my odds.

> *"The thing that drives you nuts in this game is not giving credit to the other guy. Now, when I go 0-for-4, I remind myself that the pitcher had performed well, I give the credit instead of tearing myself apart."*
>
> —Carl Yastremski

Workaholics are the athletes of the business world; in fact, many of us competed at sports in school. The same competitive drive that enabled us to excel at that level now propels us into the arena of commerce. However, business is not a game of well-defined rules; it's hard to tell teammates from competitors; it's even harder to tell who's winning; and there's no such thing as a final score. Frustrated by this state of uncertainty, you may redouble your effort to win at all costs, and in the end wind up beating yourself.

Reflections:

The key to success in any field is accepting yourself as you are—good points and bad—without reservation. If you're passed over for a promotion or lose out on a big contract, it doesn't mean you've had a bad day; it means the other fellow had a great day. If you miss out on a sales or productivity award, it doesn't mean you lost, it means someone else won. If you don't bat 1,000, neither does anyone else. Just keep swinging; you'll get your share of hits.

Every time I swing, I'm that much closer to a hit.

"We need a calculus of potentiality rather than one of probability."
—Ruth Nanda Cushen

No one would dispute the winning record of Red Auerbach, former coach of the Boston Celtics, who had a knack for getting his athletes to play over their heads. He won more world championships than any other coach in any professional sport. But when asked his formula for success, Auerbach said, "I don't look at the numbers. You can't measure the size of a ballplayer's heart." Sound advice from a man who really knows the score.

Reflections:

In the game of business, we workaholics never take our eyes off the numbers. We enjoy playing the odds, taking calculated, short-term risks, hedging our bets, trying for a decisive win. But this approach is shortsighted in that it places too much emphasis on the numbers and not enough on the people who make the numbers happen. The result is a plan that looks good on paper but does not score in the marketplace where the human element counts. Sooner or later we find ourselves saying, "Time out!"

Today I'll make a special point of telling the people at work how much I count on them.

"The road to success is always under construction."

—Anthony Robbins

Less than twenty years ago, the average executive expected to spend his or her entire career with two, possibly three, firms; today the figure is more like seven firms. Consider your own career: chances are there have been several forks on your road to success. At each junction, you have reappraised your goals, and your job, before setting out on a new direction. But no matter how far or fast you've traveled, you've never felt completely successful, have you? You've never felt like you've arrived because success is not a destination, it's a direction.

Reflections:

You may know that you're successful because your accountants, lawyers, and publicists say you are. But knowing it and *feeling* it are two different things. Instead of feeling successful, many high achievers feel tense and uneasy because they can never reach the exit ramp where the sign says, "Welcome to Success." There's always one more bend in the road, one more mile marker, and one more tollbooth. The farther you go, the higher the toll you pay. Are you sure you're going in the right direction?

A successful day is one in which I take time to grow spiritually.

"I have found that it is much easier to make a success in life than to make a success of one's life."

—G. W. Follin

The Spanish galleons of the fifteenth and sixteenth centuries carried as ballast cobblestones, to be used in paving the streets of their New World settlements. On the return voyage, the cobblestones, were replaced with bricks made of gold bullion; thus was born the myth that the streets of the New World were paved with gold. Like the conquistadors, we can choose a course that promises riches, success, and happiness, or we can turn our backs on Golconda and set out on a voyage of inner discovery.

Reflections:

We live in a secular world that gauges our success by the neighborhood we live in, the car we drive, the country club we join. If we follow the course laid out for us by society, we become ships without ballast, tossing and turning amid the shifting currents of public opinion. Yet some of the country's most successful executives—the majority of the Fortune 500 presidents—anchor their lives by regular attendance at their house of worship. These high-powered, busy executives are 60 percent more likely than the rest of the population to attend regular devotions, says *Fortune* magazine.

I'm going to volunteer at church or temple and share some of what I have received.

"*God is the tangential point between zero and infinity.*"

—Alfred Jarry

In less than forty-five years, our calculating speed rose from that of the slide rule to that of a computer that operates in nanoseconds. A nanosecond is a billionth of a second and has the same relationship to a second that a second has to thirty years. In other words, our speed of calculation increased 500,000 times in the life span of most of today's executives. We are approaching the "ultimate answer" at the speed of light. But our Higher Power will not, cannot, be reduced to the final integer in our cosmic equation.

Reflections:

Workaholics approach prayer in a cool, rational manner. We probe the will of our Higher Power as if prayer were some kind of spiritual formula. Ours is a calculating, intellectual form of prayer; yet, we expect our Higher Power to respond emotionally, to love us, and feel pity for us. The truth is, our intellects cannot sense that Power's will the way our emotions can. Instead of probing, we need to praise and thank. To experience the presence of a Higher Power in our lives, we have to approach it with the same emotional intensity we expect it to feel for us.

I praise you, Higher Power, and thank you for all you've done for me.

> "Having and being are two fundamental modes of experience, the respective strengths of which determine the differences between the characters of individuals."
>
> —Erich Fromm

Our culture places a great deal of emphasis on having or owning things. We surround ourselves with the trappings of success—the big house with a three-car garage, foreign sports car, country club membership, and vacation condo. Psychoanalyst Erich Fromm notes that our emphasis on ownership is so pervasive we assume the essence of "being" is "having"; if we have nothing, we are nothing. We even say, "Have a nice day," instead of "Make it a nice day."

Reflections:

True happiness is not being satisfied with what we have; it's being satisfied with who we are. It's being free of the hold that our possessions exert over us, the needless, senseless fears and anxieties that grip us whenever we must have things in our grip to feel satisfied. True happiness is the ability to make each day a nice day.

"All plenty which is not my God is poverty to me" (Augustine of Hippo).

"The pride of the dying rich raises the loudest laugh in hell."

—John Foster

In the investment world, he is known as the wizard of Omaha, a financial genius who turned $9,800 into a multi-billion dollar fortune. Yet Warren Buffet is a down-to-earth, genial midwesterner who still lives in the house he bought as a newly-wed. He does not own a calculator or computer, and he prepares his own income tax return. One of the keys to Warren Buffet's success is his ability to see through the numbers to a company's underlying strengths or weaknesses. He looks for intrinsic value.

Reflections:

Warren Buffet's own value system is such that he has allowed each shareholder of his investment company, Berkshire Hathaway, to specify a favorite charity to receive $2 for each share owned. In his own case, Buffet is leaving the bulk of his fortune to a foundation he has established. Warren Buffet knows you can't take it with you, so he's sending it on ahead.

Success is not a matter of how high I live, but how high I give.

AUGUST 29

*"They intoxicate themselves with work
so they won't see how they really are."*
—Aldous Huxley

If money were the only way we kept score in the game of business, it would be far easier to deal with the issue of self-esteem. After all, the size of your paycheck is largely a private matter; others can only guess at how well you're doing. But there are other, highly visible ways of keeping score that are troublesome: your title, the number of people reporting to you, the size of your office, your company car, your parking stall, and the competitor who mockingly says, "I've got your number."

Reflections:

A preoccupation with status symbols is a sign that we look to others for self-validation. When that happens, we lose touch with our own feelings and innermost needs. We are driven not so much by a need to succeed as by a need to avoid criticism or failure in the eyes of others. When it comes to recognition and rewards, 10 percent concerns how you make it and 90 percent how you take it.

The most important point about success is that it's not a matter of counting points.

"Round numbers are always fake."
—Samuel Johnson

To a workaholic, it might seem hard to believe, but the average investor spends only nine minutes reading an annual report. That's it. Nine minutes. They're only interested in the top-line numbers. They glance at the photos, read the captions, skim the president's letter, and try to decipher a few tables. By whatever means they choose, they all measure one thing: success or failure. No one cares who came in second. We're obsessed with being number one.

Reflections:

When it comes to numbers, we workaholics are different. We're preoccupied, distracted, and mesmerized by numbers. We round them, plot them, chart them, and project them until we figure out a way to be number one. But our obsession with keeping score frustrates us because no one can be number one across the board. For every asset, there is a liability, for every success a setback. Each time you round off a number, remind yourself that there's no such thing as perfection.

I need more time in contemplation and less in calculation.

"A billion dollars isn't what it used to be."

—Nelson Bunker Hunt

Every industry has them: the annual salary surveys published by the trade journals in twelve-point boldface type for all the world to see, and for you to wince at what all those high mucky-mucks rake in. Hold on, isn't that so and so, the guy who started in the bull pen with you right out of college? *He* can't be making that kind of money, can he? Not *him!* But he is, and so are all those other executives whose salaries call into question your own self-worth. How do you handle the news?

Reflections:

No matter how much you earn, there is always someone somewhere who is more successful. But numbers never tell the whole story. In the game of life, the greatest successes can't be reduced to a figure on a paycheck stub. As Montaigne said, "We are all of us richer than we think." If you count all your blessings, there won't be room for them on your paycheck stub.

Instead of reading the salary surveys, I'll spend some time looking at the family photo album.

SEPTEMBER

Anxiety

Our need for control and absolute certainty makes us averse to risk. We live in a heightened state of stress, always on the alert. We'd rather work, work, work than risk, risk, risk. We need to develop a sense of courage and a deep, abiding faith in the goodness of our Higher Power's plan for our lives.

SEPTEMBER 1

"The diseases of the mind are more destructive than those of the body."
—Marcus Tullius Cicero

As early as 1956, Hans Selye a physician, showed that stress affects the body's chemistry and its ability to ward off illness. Numerous other clinicians have shown that stress plays a role in everything from asthma, ulcers, allergies, migraine headaches, hypertension, arthritis, and cardiopulmonary diseases. Some doctors now say that 50 to 80 percent of all health disorders are stress related.

Reflections:

The person most prone to stress-related disorders is a perfectionist whose rigidity makes it difficult to adapt to change. These people have a great need for autonomy and control over every aspect of their life, and their unrealistic expectations create a state of chronic anxiety. Does that sound like anyone you know?

I may be powerless, but I'm never helpless.

SEPTEMBER 2

"Sadness is almost never anything but a form of fatigue."

—André Gide

There are actually two types of stress: eustress and distress. Eustress is the exhilaration we feel in performing an enjoyable task that challenges us somewhat, mentally or physically. All of us need a certain amount of eustress to do our best. But in a threatening situation, we move into a state of distress, or alarm, and all the body's defenses mobilize. Many workaholics have shifted over time from a state of eustress to chronic distress as their work load increases. The change is so gradual that they don't realize it until physical symptoms of anxiety appear.

Reflections:

You are more susceptible to illness when you're tired, run down, and stressed out. Under stress, the body mobilizes oxygen-rich red blood cells for flight or fight. Your white blood cell count drops as you secrete adrenalin and hydrocortisone into your immune system. Anxiety also increases the triglycerides and cholesterol in the bloodstream, which can lead to narrowing of the arteries, increased blood pressure, and longer-term cardiopulmonary disorders. When was your last physical exam?

To preserve my health, I have to relax my mind every day.

"The greatest danger, that of losing one's own self, may pass off quietly as if it were nothing."
—Søren Kierkegaard

A cartoon in the Minneapolis *Star & Tribune* captured one paradox of success. It showed a doctor saying to a junior executive: "Congratulations, your blood pressure has reached middle management level." Does the price you're paying for success include a heightened pulse rate, shortness of breath, a pounding heart, stiff muscles, upset stomach, and sleepless nights? The long-term effects of stress on our cardiovascular and immune systems can be life threatening.

Reflections:

We all need a certain amount of stress to become the best that we can be. However, we can only maintain peak performance at any activity for a short period of time, normally about forty minutes, before we must rest. If the stress remains unabated, or other problems occur, we cannot fully relax. As part of your coping strategy, become aware of your biorhythms and recognize when to take positive steps to recuperate. Go for a walk, meditate, listen to music, or whatever it takes to break the stress cycle.

I'm going to take a few minutes on my lunch hour to meditate.

SEPTEMBER 4

"Learn not to sweat the small stuff."
—Dr. Kenneth Greenspan

A study conducted by the American Management Association showed 50 percent of top management may fall into the coronary-prone lifestyle category. Another study by the American Management Society reported that the majority of managers experienced burnout at their present jobs. Whether the problem is heart disease or losing heart, the underlying cause is stress. People who suffer most from stress are those who are obsessed with details, those who feel chronically rushed at work, and perfectionists, reported pollster Lou Harris.

Reflections:

"Whirl is king," said Aristophanes, nearly three centuries ago. Today we whirl about like spinning tops, afraid that if we stop for a moment, we'll lose our balance and topple. We worry over every detail, fret over the slightest imperfection, and dizzy ourselves with mindless activity. We forget that, unless we slow down and come to rest, we can't lead truly balanced lives. When was the last time you set aside three solid hours for uninterrupted reflection on your lifestyle?

In the whirl of daily business activities I need prayer to maintain my sense of balance.

"If my boss calls, get his name."
—Cartoon pinned to the bulletin board
of an acquired company

U.S. industry is undergoing a massive restructuring. In one recent quarter, there were almost $100 billion worth of corporate takeovers involving publicly held companies and billions more involving privately held firms. Countless other companies down-sized to bolster their bottom lines. No wonder 30,000 people a year attend seminars on coping with job stress and many more buy books on the subject; perhaps you are one of them.

Reflections:

As workaholics, our automatic approach to dealing with stress is to simply work harder. But in many cases the forces of the marketplace are beyond the control of any one person, so that working harder serves no useful purpose. One way to cope with stress is stretching exercises and moderate physical activity, such as walking, swimming, golf, tennis, and aerobic dancing. How long has it been since you had a physical? Why not ask your doctor to prescribe a physical fitness program to help you work off the stress of your job?

My first job is to remain strong enough, physically, to handle the stress and strain of my job.

"Every new adjustment is a crisis in self-esteem."

—Eric Hoffer

One of the things contributing to your workaholism may be a fear of losing your job. After all, more than half the Fortune 1,000 have cut staff in the last decade, so you have legitimate reason to be concerned. However, in today's marketplace loss of a job has more to do with fundamental changes in the economy than with individual performance. In fact, 70 percent of those laid off by the Fortune 1000 had received outstanding evaluations in their last review. They were fired for reasons beyond their control. Fortunately, unemployment doesn't bear the stigma it once did. You can hold your head up high during your job hunt.

Reflections:

Loss of a job can be devastating because your identity is so closely linked to your work. The initial reaction may be depression and anxiety, coupled with feelings of betrayal and anger. Confused, shaken, and cut off from co-workers you have come to rely on for support, you may not know where to turn. That's why, if you think your job is at risk, you should prepare now for a career move, while you're still employed. Update your resume; start networking; join a support group at your church or community center. The sooner you start looking, the better.

In the final analysis, I've always been self-employed.

*"All life is the management of risk, not
its elimination."*
—Walter Wriston

Tighter budgets, thinner staffs, fierce competition, buyouts, buybacks, mergers, and acquisitions—the harsh realities of today's business world can raise anyone's anxiety level. You may begin to doubt your abilities, second-guess yourself, and hesitate to act decisively. In a crisis, your tendency may be to reduce the risk by avoiding bold moves; instead of turning the company around, you turn yourself around, and around, and around—searching for a creative solution to your problems.

Reflections:

In a crisis, there will be plenty of people willing to give you advice, much of it negative, cautious, and demoralizing. Embittered by the company's setbacks, they may blame you and reject your every proposal. Their attitude seems to be "Seeing is believing"; but in a crisis, just the opposite is true—"Believing is seeing." You have to believe in yourself in order to envision the bold, creative moves necessary to turn a crisis around. Confidence is the catalyst that turns setbacks into success.

I believe I'm up to the creative challenges I face.

"Ambition having reached the summit, longs to descend."
—Pierre Corneille

Any well-run company expects more of its managers than is humanly possible. The only way you can cope with the anxiety level is to learn how to delegate. To encourage its managers to delegate, Procter & Gamble tells them they're ready for a promotion when they've trained their replacement. Like many other leading companies, Procter & Gamble rewards those who know how to bring out the best in others. They consider delegation a key management skill.

Reflections:

How would your subordinates rate you as a delegator and developer? Would they say you'd rather do it yourself and make sure it's done right than take time out of your busy schedule to train them? Do you hoard essential information? Do you make clear what's expected and the due date? Do you show your appreciation for their efforts and give them feedback on their performance? If your next promotion were up to your subordinates, do you think you'd get it?

Every task should be delegated to the lowest level of competence.

SEPTEMBER 9

"Drive thy business; let it not drive thee."

—Benjamin Franklin

During the business day, you probably work on a number of projects; their files spread out on your desk. However, if a file sits untouched on your desk for more than a week, take another look at your paperwork practices. A cluttered desktop is a sign of confused priorities. You're doing too many things at once. The root cause of this problem is a need for total control, and the predictable result is anxiety. Every file on your desk is a potential stressor, a reminder of an unfinished job. As the stacks grow, you can easily lose track of what's in them, adding to your anxiety.

Reflections:

Much of the anxiety you feel at work stems from controlling too many projects at the same time. As a first step in letting go, why not remove from your desktop any files that do not require attention today? Get yourself an accordion-fold suspending file to store papers you'll need later in the week. Then file anything of value that you don't need this week in your desk drawer. The rest of the paperwork goes in the round file.

Today I'll rearrange my desk and my thinking.

"Don't agonize. Organize."
—Florence R. Kennedy

The average executive spends thirty-six anxious minutes a day looking for misplaced files. Since no one search lasts more than a few minutes, you may not notice how much time is wasted in this way. But over the course of the day the lost time and mounting frustration add to the general feeling of stress. Confusion piles on top of confusion, until 5:00 p.m., when your desk is a jumble of files, phone memos, and unopened mail. In frustration, you may turn off your computer, lock your desk drawer, and leave your office in total disarray.

Reflections:

Mastering deskmanship can lower your stress level, increase your efficiency, and bolster your enthusiasm for work. When you receive mail, decide immediately whether to toss, refer it to someone else, act on it, or file for future reference. If you file it, indicate a date for purging it. If you act on it, be sure to end your work on the project each day at a natural breaking point so you can pick up where you left off easily. Give yourself ten minutes at the end of the day to straighten up your desk so you can start the next day off with the right frame of mind.

At the end of each day, I'll spend ten minutes preparing for tomorrow.

SEPTEMBER 11

*"An essential aspect of creativity is not
being afraid to fail."*

—Edwin Rand

In psyching yourself up for a big presentation,
it's possible to try too hard. When that happens, you
can become self-conscious, anxious, and uptight.
That self-critical voice within you disrupts your
thoughts with feedback even as you speak: "You're
losing them," "They're three pages ahead of you. . . ."
Confidence shaken, you lose your spontaneity, and
your wooden remarks and body language signal to
others your distress. You are unable to deliver a
peak performance.

Reflections:

A certain amount of anxiety is normal when
you anticipate an important presentation. But it can
become abnormal when you focus on yourself instead of on the subject of your presentation. If you
find yourself getting uptight, try to recall a similar
situation in which you gave a peak performance.
See yourself making that presentation again. Hear
yourself speaking. Relive that moment of achievement. Then take another look at the material you're
about to present. Become more familiar with it, and
you'll feel more confident in presenting it.

*I have to concentrate on my material instead of on
myself.*

SEPTEMBER 12

"It's not appropriate in a corporation to admit your concerns or problems. I think that's the major executive crisis—their inability to have one."

—John De Luca

Art curators recently unveiled a long-hidden sketch of Cleopatra concealed beneath the matting papers on the reverse side of a painting of the Egyptian Queen created by Michelangelo nearly 400 years ago. The new sketch reveals a pensive, pouting Cleopatra in sharp contrast to the controlled passions in the finished work. In a sense, we, too, have a pensive, anxious side to our personalities, which we conceal from the rest of the world much of the time. In fact, we may conceal its existence from ourselves and pretend everything is fine, when we are consumed by fear.

Reflections:

When we expose our fears for what they are, they are never as bad as we imagined. They are sketchy, raw, undeveloped spectral images lacking in vivid, lifelike colors. Why not face up to your fears and deal with them today? Ask yourself which fear has been dominating your thinking, and turn it to the wall. Improve your frame of mind.

I'm going to put my fear behind me.

"Often, the thing we fear most is being ourselves."

—Bob Larrañaga

If you've ever collated a slide show, you may know the best slides have glass mounts. A glass mount holds the slide snugly in focus and prevents it from warping and jamming the mechanism. Like 35-mm slides in a carousel projector, our self-image changes many times in the course of a day: trainer, team leader, assistant, boss. But these images aren't glass mounted, and if we try to do too much, they will jam and burn out under the high-intensity lamp called *stress*.

Reflections:

Most workaholics suffer from a mild case of FUD (fear, uncertainty, doubt). We fear that if people saw us as we really are, they wouldn't like us. We're uncertain of our own abilities, and in our self-doubt we take on more and more in order to appear perfect. But we can't live up to all the image we're projecting and eventually must change our behavior or burn out.

I'm going to take on only one job at a time.

"There's no such thing as 'zero risk.'"
—William Driver

Fear of rejection is a palpable presence peering over the shoulder of every workaholic who submits a written proposal, makes a flip-chart presentation, or conducts a slide show for management. We fear disapproval because our egos are so closely linked with what we do for a living. We take a criticism of our work as a criticism of our selves. Confused, we ignore the fact that perfection is impossible. Some people judge us critically because of their own subjective beliefs. Others may find fault with our work for good sound reasons. But no one thinks we're perfect.

Reflections:

Why not deal with fear of rejection the way top salespeople do? Rejection is a fact of life when you're making cold calls, but the best salespeople turn it to their advantage. They figure out how many no's they hear for every yes, and divide that number into the value of a sale to find out what every rejection is worth to them. The point is, no one is perfect, and every mistake is a valuable learning experience. Remember what Thomas Watson, Sr., said: "If you're not succeeding, double your rate of failure."

I have to overcome my fears and take risks in order to succeed.

SEPTEMBER 15

*"Enough then of worrying about tomor-
row."*

—Mark 6:34

At the farewell party for a retiring workaholic,
the guest of honor was asked for a few parting words
of wisdom. After the usual perfunctory remarks, he
hesitated long enough to take in the audience in a
sweeping gaze, cleared his throat, and said, "You
know, for forty years I believed what the company
said about our problems and opportunities being
one and the same. Don't you believe it—the problems go home with you at night."

Reflections:

Intellectual work has a halo effect that extends
beyond the office. We take it home with us at night.
Our minds return to unresolved problems; our
dreams focus on business concerns; and our subconscious second-guesses every decision. To minimize
the halo effect of work, use the trip home at night to
change the direction of your thinking. One workaholic tunes his car radio to a "Golden Oldies" station and recalls when times were more carefree.
Another works the crossword puzzle in the paper.
And a third stops at a health club to work off the
day's stress. Experiment till you find an approach
that works for you.

*I have enough problems at work without bringing
them home, too.*

"To be a prophet, it is sufficient to be a pessimist."

—Elsa Triolet

Every pessimist has his or her day. Sooner or later, the bottom will fall out of the stock market again, the economy will take a drubbing, your business will develop cash flow problems, and a competitor will undercut your price. And, yes, eventually the Four Horsemen of Apocalypse will appear on the horizon. If you look long enough and hard enough, you can find something worrisome to confirm your worst suspicions.

Reflections:

One of your great strengths as a workaholic is your vigilance: you're constantly on the lookout for the early warning signals that can spell trouble for your business. But what about the positive developments, the upbeat news, the favorable trends?— are you considering them, too? Or do losses loom larger than gains? Most people are so risk averse that, given fifty-fifty odds, they will bet only if they stand to win twice as much as they can lose. As a result, they never take a chance on success. Are you a pessimist or realist?

Today I'm going to take a realistic look at my odds of succeeding.

"If something can go wrong, it will go wrong, when you least expect it."
—Murphy's law

There is a natural tendency for our self-talk to become negative, due to a statistical factor called "regression to the mean." That is, in any series of random events clustering around an average, an extraordinary event is apt to be followed by a more ordinary event. Regression suggests that a great performance will be followed by a poor one. But our subconscious doesn't know this; all it knows is that, right after it congratulates us on a good job, we screw up. So it decides there's no sense congratulating us—we'll only mess up the next time. The result is, we stop reveling in our victories and begin criticizing our failures. We undermine our self-confidence.

Reflections:

Fortunately, we have a powerful advantage over that anxious, self-doubting voice within. Although it is inaudible, we can actually hear ourselves speaking aloud about our hopes and dreams. We can reinforce our positive, confidence-building thoughts by voicing them and drowning out that critical voice that distorts our thoughts. How long has it been since you gave yourself a pep talk?

I'm going to make this an above-average day.

"Some kinds of success are indistinguishable from panic."

—Edgar Degas

"The good news is, I won the sales contest; the bad news is, they raised my quota" ... "I have a no-limit expense account, but I live on Bromo, Big Macs, and pizza" ... "I saw every one of my son's Little League games—on videotape." Listen to workaholics talk, and you get the feeling they're hard driven, not hard driving. Their work seems devoid of choice. They speak in the anxious, breathless tones of someone hyperventilating. They never seem to have time to pause and reflect on their success.

Reflections:

Why not take a few moments now to list some of your biggest accomplishments? As you write them down, try to visualize and recreate the moment of greatest exhilaration. How did you feel? What emotions did you experience? Take your time and enjoy the feeling; there's no need to rush through it in order to get on to something else. You've earned the right to relax.

The only success worth achieving is self-actualization.

SEPTEMBER 19

"It is always safe to assume, not that the old way is wrong, but that there may be a better way."
—Henry Harrower

No doubt, computers are highly effective, labor-saving devices. They can be programmed with an appointment calendar, phone book, PERT chart, sales forecast, budget, and electronic spreadsheet. But at times it may feel like those electric cords from your computer are hard-wired to your nerve endings. Nothing so frustrates a high-strung workaholic as a computer that goes haywire just when you need it most. Suddenly your high-tech office is a high-stress office.

Reflections:

If you're not computer literate, the average software manual reads like Sanskrit. But the cause of your anxiety is not so much the programmer's instructions as it is the instructions you give yourself. You raise your stress level when you say, "I can't handle this" or "I'm too old to change." Identify the areas you find difficult, and break them down into manageable steps. Then tell yourself, "This is a great learning experience," and chances are it will be. Program yourself to succeed, and boot up that computer program!

I'm ready to master the computer.

"The great end of life is not knowledge, but action."
—Thomas Henry Huxley

All decisions involve some risk and attempting to eliminate all risk poses a new one: inertia. In today's fast-changing world, nothing stands still for long. The most thoroughly researched plans are partially obsolete the moment they're launched. Like a guidance missile fired in the general direction of a target, they require mid-course corrections as feedback is received. Once you've defined your target and calculated your risks, build into your plan a feedback mechanism, and launch it.

Reflections:

It's possible to become so engrossed in the planning process that you lose sight of the fact that the real test of your plans is results. If all your facts were laid end to end, they wouldn't reach a decision: only you can do that. Only you can take action and bring your plan to life. Gathering more and more facts can be a way of procrastinating and forestalling the need to act on your plan. Analysis lead to paralysis.

In order to succeed, I have to act on my plans.

*"I've had a lot of troubles in my life,
most of which never happened."*
—Mark Twain

According to the Roper Organization, about 75 percent of all workers say their jobs are stressful, and more than half reported "moderate" to "a lot" of stress in the past two weeks. For many workaholics, anxiety is a daily fact of life. Without diminishing the seriousness of the problem, it is important to realize many of our worries are unfounded. A doctor, who recorded patients' worries, reported that forty percent of the worries never happened, 30 percent had already happened, 12 percent were about imaginary illnesses, and 10 percent of the worries were about someone else. Only 8 percent were well founded.

Reflections:

We workaholics are chronic worriers. When business is going well, we say, "Things could be better"; and when our business is soft, we say, "I knew it couldn't continue." We constantly scan the horizon for the approach of the Four Horsemen of Apocalypse. To complicate matters, we can usually find some evidence to confirm our worst fears. In fact, our anxiety can cause us to overreact in a crisis and become a self-fulfilling prophecy of doom.

The best way to predict the future is to invent it.

"Laughter builds strength in the soul, and without muscle in the soul, you can't face the tough things in life."
—Glenn Cunningham

In the early stages of burnout, a sense of lethargy and chronic fatigue sets in. You can see it in the way depressed people carry themselves: shoulders stooped, arms immobile at their sides, head downcast, facial muscles drooping. Their physiology reflects their mood. If you sense these changes coming over you, keep in mind that you are the master of your moods. No one can make you feel depressed. You do it to yourself. One way to break out of your depression is to start acting happy.

Reflections:

Every mental state has a corresponding physical state. Biofeedback studies demonstrate that we can alter our moods by flexing our muscles. For example, fear constricts our breathing, so throwing your shoulders back and breathing deeply can help you feel more relaxed and confident. Anxiety wrinkles our brow; but smiling makes us feel happy, and laughing actually releases endorphins—natural tranquilizers—in our brain. If you're feeling nervous and tense, why not enjoy a good joke book tonight?

I'm going to laugh myself into a good mood.

"Our greatest glory is not in never failing, but in rising every time we fall."
—Confucius

The only artificial structure visible from the moon is the Great Wall of China. Built in the fifteenth century, it stands today as a reminder of how fear of the unknown can imprison us. Before the wall's construction, China was the most advanced civilization in the world. A flotilla of 317 Chinese ships with 37,000 sailors under Ching Ho's command took seven voyages of discovery throughout the Indian Ocean and China Sea. The largest naval expedition in history, it returned without tribute or plunder, whereupon the emperor burned the entire fleet and walled in his subjects, rather than risk another costly voyage of discovery.

Reflections:

Are you open-minded and willing to take affordable risks? Nothing great has ever been achieved without taking some risk. Often the greatest opportunities involve incalculable risks because when something has never been done before there is no way to gauge the odds of success or failure. The greatest risk of all is to not risk anything.

One sign of open-mindedness is my willingness to read the "alternative press."

> *"The only real security that a man can have in this world is a reserve of knowledge, experience and ability."*
> —Henry Ford

The idea that financial security gives us the freedom to do as we wish doesn't square with the facts. We actually trade our freedom for financial security: the greater our need for security, and the greater our dependence on material possessions, the less freedom we have. The things we rely on become binding chains, and we become our own jailers. The castle that provides our security also walls us in.

Reflections:

"The true test of success," according to Michael Korda, "is the degree to which one is able to isolate oneself from others." It almost sounds like a prison sentence, doesn't it? Yet the cell block Korda refers to is executive row in a major corporation, where security cameras monitor the reception room doors and admittance is restricted to those with security codes. The occupants sit in stern and solemn isolation, dine in private splendor, and travel in private jets, guarded by their retinue. In a sense, they're prisoners of success. The same can be said of anyone who exchanges freedom for security. True freedom is the letting go of all attachments.

The only real security comes from within.

SEPTEMBER 25

"I discovered that there is only one way to handle fear: Go out and scare yourself."

—Hugh Downs

As a young man, television star Hugh Downs was timid and shy. But he learned to overcome his fears and leave his stage fright behind, en route to becoming one of television's premiere performers. Like Hugh Downs, all of us grapple with fear in one form or another: fear of rejection, pain, loss, responsibility. The greatest fear is a nameless fear because we can't cope with a problem until we correctly identify it. Naming our fears is the first step toward gaining power over them.

Reflections:

Every worthwhile goal involves risk, so it is only natural to feel some fear. But once you've identified the cause of your fear, you can deal with it. If the cause of your fear is competition, chances are you're not the only one with these feelings; your adversaries are probably worried, too. After all, you are a formidable competitor. When fear enters in, the competition thins out, and the field is left to people like you who walk in the direction of their fear. Fear can become your ally, pointing the way to a success few others dare to achieve.

Give me the courage to go out and scare myself today.

"Worry is the interest paid on trouble before it becomes due."
—Deacon William Ralph Inge

As the chief executive officer of Hewlett-Packard, John Young has been a staunch advocate of productivity enhancement techniques. To get his company moving faster, he has equipped engineers with computerized expert systems and computerized engineering databases. His goal is to reduce by half the breakeven time, or the interval between product concept and profitability. Despite his zeal for driving Hewlett-Packard, John Young manages to keep his own speed on cruise control.

Reflections:

How is it that a hard-charging executive like John Young can leave people with the impression that he's "cool, competent, confident, and cheerful?" How does he minimize self-induced stress? To quote *Fortune* magazine, "he practices what he calls just-in-time worrying: not bothering with a task until he absolutely must." "If you worry too soon, he says, "things will change in the interim so you end up having to deal with them twice." Are you worrying twice as much as you have to?

I'm going to practice just-in-time worrying.

"It takes as much energy to wish as it does to plan."

—Eleanor Roosevelt

One sure way to raise your anxiety level is to keep multiple calendars: a pocket calendar, a desk calendar, a to-do list and a pert chart. Without having all the activities listed together in a single source, it's easy to overlook something or schedule two things at once; then cross your fingers and hope someone cancels out or delays a project.

Reflections:

Entering every activity in one calendar forces you to prioritize projects and make a realistic appraisal of the time needed, especially if the calendar divides the day into quarter-hour increments for planning purposes. Why not start each day by adding to your calendar a quote from this book or your daily devotional, a reminder of your goal to manage time wisely?

My goal is to do one thing at a time and to do it well.

"Archie doesn't know how to worry without getting upset."
—Edith Bunker in "All In The Family"

A 4,000-year-old Sumerian tablet lists a dozen drug prescriptions; the ancient Egyptians expanded the list to eight hundred; and the Romans opened the first drugstores. Today, according to *Dowline* magazine, pharmaceutical products represent a multibillion-dollar industry. We take, for example, 20,000 tons of aspirin a day, almost one tablet for every single person in the country. But the largest single category is stimulants and sedatives. Over 2.4 million people regularly take Valium and related tranquilizers. The size and scope of the drug industry is symptomatic of the stress faced by business-people today.

Reflections:

We all are subject to mood swings. A simple change in our diet, such as drinking caffeine or eating sweets, can alter our biochemistry and our moods. A change in sleep habits or work schedule can also trigger a sudden change in mood. In fact, our mood shifts throughout the day in synchronization with our biorhythms. However, when a depression lasts for a prolonged period, the tendency is to medicate yourself. Before reaching this state, remember that faith is worry that has said its prayers.

Instead of popping a pill, I'll pop a prayer.

"I fear one lies more to one's self than anyone else."

—Lord Byron

One of the biggest factors feeding your sense of anxiety may be your diet. If you drink more than three cups of coffee a day, you're disrupting your metabolic rate and sleep pattern. If you snack on sweets, you're elevating your blood sugar level and setting yourself up for a hypoglycemic reaction, or midday meltdown. If your power lunches are rich and spicy, all that extra salt causes your body to retain excess water and raises your blood pressure. It's no wonder that by the end of the day you feel like a zombie.

Reflections:

By itself, a stressful job can deplete your body of the vitamin C and the B-complex vitamins that have a calming effect on the nervous system. But when you try to cope with job pressures by getting a quick fix from coffee, sweets, or snacks, you're in for a letdown. By adjusting your diet and supplementing it with multivitamins, you'll be better able to cope with the stress.

A healthy diet can give me a healthier outlook, too.

"More powerful than the will to win is the courage to begin."

—Anonymous

For many workaholics, nicotine is the drug of choice. Hard-driving, chain-smoking executives light up to steady their nerves, relax, and enjoy a break in the work routine. But the long-term effects of smoking are anything but calming. Researchers estimate that each pack of cigarettes takes 20 minutes off your life. If you smoke two packs a day, you double your chances of dying from a heart attack or lung cancer. One in every six deaths this year will be linked to cigarette smoking.

Reflections:

Chances are, you've tried going cold turkey before. But each time you've quit something has happened and your willpower has gone up in smoke. The fact is, smoking is not a "bad habit," it is (in the words of the Surgeon General) an *addiction* to nicotine. You may need the help of a doctor to withdraw. Don't wait until "things are slow at work," "the big presentation is behind you," or "your vacation." You may run out of breath before you run out of excuses.

I'm going to quit smoking for good.

OCTOBER

Moderation

We workaholics tend to do everything to excess. We need to develop a sense of moderation and the self-discipline to relax and restore our physical and mental energies. We have to learn to be content with ourselves and to exercise restraint in the ways we spend our time and money. In order to monitor our progress, we need to take inventory daily, examining our strengths and weaknesses, motives and behaviors.

OCTOBER 1

"Leisure is the most challenging respon-
sibility a man can be offered."
—William Russell

One definition of stress is an overactive mind in an underactive body. If you work at a desk, you're prone to anxiety, simply because you don't have a chance to work off the stress that accumulates during the business day. Your blood pressure may be 140 over 80; your EKG may be normal and your total cholesterol level may be under 200. But, if you're not taking time out from work, sooner or later your fun meter will be in the red zone.

Reflections:

We all need mental and physical breaks to allow our subconscious to mull things over, play with an idea, gain fresh insights, and maybe even question why we're working on a problem in the first place. For some, the time spent in the outdoors is a tonic for mind and body. For others, the answer may lie elsewhere. It may mean enrolling in an adult education class on auto repair or photography. It could be volunteering at a local hospital. The idea is to find some activity far removed from what you do at work.

I'm going to spend the time on something totally unrelated to work.

OCTOBER 2

"A yawn is a silent scream."
—Oscar Wilde

You push yourself to the limits of exhaustion and close your mind to the pain. Your legs grow stiff, and the small of your back aches from sitting too long in one position. You leave your desk only to get a cup of coffee, or to splash water on your face in the washroom. You continue to work long after your spirit has given out. You doze off in a meeting, rub your eyes just as a client makes a key point, and ignore the silent screams of a body in protest—your body.

Reflections:

You simply cannot make good decisions when you're overtired. If you must work long days for a period of time, take breaks during the day for "deskercises." Let your chin fall toward your chest, breathing deeply, your head tilted back until your chin points upward. Hold a few seconds and exhale, lowering your head to normal position. With shoulders relaxed, roll your head toward your right shoulder and breathe deeply. Repeat to left side. With your head held high, roll your shoulders forward and down, then backward and down. Finally, extend your arms forward, chest high. Turn your palms outward and hold a few seconds. You've just stretched your muscles and mind.

I'm going to "work out" my problems at my desk.

"Workaholics commit slow suicide by refusing to allow the child inside them to play."

—Laurence Susser

We all have a greater capacity for pain than pleasure. Pleasure is a fleeting, heightened experience that can't be sustained without becoming painful. However, pain may be enduring, and since it is not optional, we learn to live with it. Sometimes, mentally blocking out pain is self-defeating. For example, if you plunge your hand into scalding water, you immediately recoil in pain; but if you put your hand in tepid water and gradually raise the temperature, you block out each small change, until the cumulative effect becomes serious. Something similar happens inside us when we accept one crushing job after another. Our blood boils.

Reflections:

As perfectionists, we take on punishing work loads to atone for our failings. We feel guilty and angry at ourselves for not living up to our impossible standards. We try to redeem ourselves with hard work. Have you given yourself permission to say no to a punishing work load? Do you accept the fact that you make mistakes? Can you recognize when you're simmering inside, or do you wait until your blood boils to do something about it?

Every ache and pain is a signal to change.

OCTOBER 4

"Not in time, place, or circumstances,
but in the man lies success."
—Charles B. Rous

Heart disease ranks number one among causes of death in America. Our sedentary work, poor eating habits, and the pressures of modern lifestyles all take their toll on our cardiovascular system. In the hustle and bustle of the big city, we're stressed out by jostling crowds, blaring traffic, and rude shopkeepers; in the suburbs, it's trains that don't run on time, organized sports that aren't organized and endless trips to the store. The stress is so endemic, it's impossible to isolate a single cause in order to alleviate it. But you can remedy the problem.

Reflections:
One of the best ways to counter the effects of stress is exercise three times a week for twenty minutes at a time. After warming up with stretching exercises, use the large muscles in a rhythmic, repetitive continuous motion that fully stretches and contracts the muscle. Your goal should be a "target heartbeat." To determine your target, deduct your age from the number 220 and take 70 to 85 percent of that figure, and you have the range in which your heart should beat per minute when exercising. Of course, it's a good idea to see your doctor first.

I'm taking responsibility for my own well-being.

"To do nothing is in every man's power."
—Samuel Johnson

There is a form of aerobic exercise all of us have the time and energy to do each day, and that is simply deep breathing. Deep breathing helps you enter a state of deep relaxation in which your brain wave pattern actually changes from the beta level of conscious thought to the deeper, slower level of alpha thought. At the same time, deep breathing oxygenates our blood and stimulates our lymph systems to slough off the toxic by-products of stress that accumulate in our bodies.

Reflections:

In his best-seller, *Unlimited Power*, Anthony Robbins recommends deep breathing exercises at least three times a day. In order to get maximum benefit, breathe in deeply from your diaphragm for a count of one, hold your breath for a count of four, and exhale for two counts. Repeat this cycle for five minutes, and at the end of the session, you'll feel relaxed, invigorated, and ready to take on new challenges.

Life begins anew with every breath I take.

"We always attract into our lives whatever we think about the most, believe in most strongly, expect at the deepest levels and/or imagine most vividly."
—Shakti Gwain

All habits, including your work habits, reside at the subconscious level so you cannot get at them solely through conscious thought and willpower. Fortunately, you have a powerful ally in your imagination, because the subconscious does not distinguish between real and imagined events. Through the power of imagination, you can picture yourself changing your work habits for the better and, in the process, discover how to relax.

Reflections:
The key to overcoming workaholism is to set fairly simple concrete goals at first, picture yourself attaining them, and focus on your goals often during the day, affirming yourself verbally. For example, you might start by visualizing yourself seated behind a cleared desk, working on one project at a time. Next, you might imagine yourself running a meeting, delegating responsibilities, and maintaining a feeling of quiet competence. Or, you might picture yourself exercising on your lunch hour each day, calling it quits at 5, or whatever other goal you'd like to achieve. If you can see it happening, it will happen.

I can see myself succeeding at my new lifestyle.

> "When we are unable to find tranquility within ourselves, it is useless to seek it elsewhere."
> —LaRochefoucauld

Intellectual work involves the manipulation of words, and symbols, which are primarily left-brain functions. In this sort of thinking, the value of our knowledge is usually a function of the mental effort needed to arrive at it. But there is another form of knowledge that we arrive at when we are relaxed. We just know it. And that is the intuitive knowledge that reposes in the right side of the brain. Although we are not conscious of the working of the right side of the brain, it is constantly processing thoughts for which there are no words.

Reflections:

In order to access our intuitive knowledge, we have to relax the left side of our brain, and the way we do that is through leisure. Leisure is not merely a matter of spare time, a holiday, a weekend, or vacation, it is also a period of quieting all conscious thoughts. Leisure does not exist for the sake of restoring our ability to work; it cannot be sought as a means to an end, or it becomes work. Leisure is an end state in which we learn our own innermost thoughts.

The original meaning of holiday was "holy day."

"There is only one success—to be able to spend your life in your own way."
—Christopher Morley

How much personal time do you have? The answer might surprise you. Let's suppose you're awake from 6:00 a.m. to 10:30 p.m. We'll figure forty-five minutes for washing and dressing and sixty minutes round trip to work. Cooking, eating, and dishwashing take ninety minutes; and household chores, such as laundry and repairs, can add thirty. Assume another sixty minutes for food and clothes shopping, dry cleaning, a haircut, the gas station, doctor, and other errands. Then add ninety minutes for family activities ranging from schoolwork and PTA to Little League and Brownies. Finally, add a 10-hour workday, and you might be lucky to have fifteen minutes to yourself each day.

Reflections:

Of the 1,440 minutes in every twenty-four-hour day, less than 5 percent may be yours to spend freely as you wish. The rest of your time is already committed. If you add something to your schedule, something else has to go. Before you make any more commitments, ask yourself what you're prepared to give up, or you may sacrifice the only time you can call your own.

I'm going to give myself the gift of a few minutes of time each day.

"If you watch a game, it's fun. If you play it, it's recreation. If you work at it, it's golf."

—Bob Hope

The impulse to play is born into us and has a vital role in the most meaningful of human activities: art, music, writing, and inventing. It's also a means for children to learn how to mimic adult behavior. Play is an outlet for socially unacceptable feelings and a way for resolving conflicts. It is spontaneous, imaginative, and somewhat chaotic in that the rules are changeable. We need a sense of play in our approach to work, an unbridled openness to change and challenge.

Reflections:

One measure of your playfulness is the amount of exercise you get each day. According to a survey of chief executive officers by Ernst & Whinney, nearly half are in very good or excellent shape, and they attribute their healthy condition to exercising about thirty minutes daily. Although the type of exercise varies with the executive's age, the most popular activities are jogging, walking, golf, tennis, and general exercise. How much exercise do you get each day?

I'm going to set aside fifteen minutes daily for aerobic exercise.

OCTOBER 10

"Sometimes the most urgent and vital thing you can do is take a complete rest."

—Ashleigh Brilliant

Do you relegate your leisure time to the weekend so that nothing interferes with your work? Do you combine your weekend fun and work—playing golf, tennis, and racquetball with clients—so you can accomplish two things at once? Do you have an extra set of season tickets for client entertaining? Like many workaholics, you've probably allowed work to encroach on your leisure time. According to a Louis Harris survey, between 1973 and 1985 "the number of leisure hours available to most Americans dropped from 26.2 to 17.7 hours a week, a loss of 8.5 hours every week, or one hour and 12 minutes a day."

Reflections:

Nowhere is it written that you have to wait for the weekends to have fun. There are all sorts of activities you can enjoy after work. You can take in a movie, play in a bridge club, host a mystery dinner, take dancing lessons, or enroll in an evening school course (one that has absolutely nothing to do with work). The spontaneity of a spur-of-the-moment night out is half the fun of it. If you're tired of the humdrum, march to the beat of a different drum. Break your routine this week. There is life after work.

I'm going to take a break in the middle of the work week.

OCTOBER 11

"Success is a marathon, not a sprint."
—Anonymous

You know you're a workaholic when you bound out of bed at 6:00 a.m. on Saturday in order to get a head start on loafing. You may start the day off with a brisk workout, but more likely you'll skip the warmup routine as a waste of time. You won't walk, you won't jog, you'll simply run with one eye on your stopwatch until you pull a muscle, injure a tendon, or hurt your back. Then, if you're like the rest of us workaholics, you'll say "That was some workout," and limp home to collapse on the couch for the rest of the day.

Reflections:

Actually, you don't have to sweat profusely or strain to exercise properly. An effective workout should take at least twenty minutes of exercise three times a week with a five-minute warmup and cooldown. If you have an hour to yourself, a simple walk at four miles per hour is excellent exercise. You burn around 400 calories and elevate your metabolism so that you continue to burn calories at a higher rate for up to four hours. Take a closer look at the road to success; it has a walking path, too.

This weekend I'm going to take a four-mile walk.

"Work does not make one rich, but round-shouldered."

—Russian proverb

Do you take less vacation than you've earned? Have you cut short any vacation due to problems at work? Do you take work on a vacation and leave a phone number where you can be reached? If so, you're not alone. According to management consultants, Goodrich and Sherwood, 83 percent of all executives take less vacation than allotted, 40 percent take work on vacation, 75 percent phone the office and 29 percent receive frequent calls from the office on their vacations. Their attitude was summed up by one CEO who surprised his staff by returning a week early. "When you've seen one castle," he said, "you've seen them all."

Reflections:

Joseph Pieper, the German philosopher, described leisure as a form of silence; a quieting of the spirit that is only possible when we are at one with ourselves and content to let things take their course. Leisure is not simply the result of spare time, a holiday, weekend, or vacation. Leisure is not a period in which we rest up for work; it is an end in itself. Leisure is letting go, a mental and spiritual liberation, an attitude akin to prayer.

This weekend I will not bring home any office work.

*"We feel guilty over pleasure, so we take
care not to get too much of it."*
—Warren Oates

The workaholic president of a major company
approached life at Mach I speed. He walked fast,
he talked fast, and when he traveled on the corporate jet he took the controls. He took the same high-
intensity approach to fun, too. For example, he
loved playing gin rummy, winning, or losing $30 to
$50 a night; but after years of keeping detailed rec-
ords of his wins and losses, he figured out he had
just about broken even. So he decided there was no
sense playing. He quit gin rummy! How about you?
Can you have fun without keeping score? Do you
have to win to be happy, or can you simply enjoy
playing?

Reflections:

For many workaholics, leisure feels like failure!
We're not accomplishing anything. If we start to enjoy time off, our conscience nags at us to return to
work. We even turn our play into work by keeping
score, playing for all the chips. It's as if there is
something sinful about pleasure and work is our
penance. The ability to enjoy time off comes when
we accept that a creative balanced life is actually the
most productive one.

*I'll prepare a list of enjoyable activities and select
one I haven't done in a long time.*

*"Let us permit nature to have her way;
she understands her business better than
we do."*
—Michel de Montaigne

One of the most peaceful leisure activities is a walk in a woodland park, trying to identify all the sights and sounds. We're reminded that nature has created 9,000 species of birds, 25,000 species of fish, and 4,500 species of mammals. But in our own genus there is only one species—*Homo sapiens.* Unlike our fellow creatures, we are not forced by environmental stress to speciate, because we control our surroundings. When we experience stress, we change our environment. Now, however, artificial factors are changing our environment in ways that add to our stress.

Reflections:

To minimize environmental stress, decorate your office with green plants and natural wall hangings. Face your desk away from doors and aisles, and place a filing cabinet between you and the traffic flow. Hang sound-absorbing drapes, use a foam pad and cover for your word processor, and lower the sound of the bell on your phone. Finally, make sure the lighting is adequate, and that the office colors are neutral.

I'm going to make my work area as close to nature as possible.

"Live your life with wide margins."
                    —Henry David Thoreau

In the play, *The Virtuoso*, by Thomas Shadwell, the curtain rises on Sir Nicholas Gimcrack making froglike swimming motions on a table. When asked if he intends to swim in the water, he replies, "Never, sir; I hate the water. I content myself with the speculative part of swimming and care not for the practical." Many workaholics take Gimcrack's approach to exercise. We buy exercise bikes and use them as clothes valets; we buy jogging outfits and wear them while watching Monday night football. The only thing we exercise is our minds.

Reflections:

Someone once described a workaholic as a machine for turning coffee into memos; we gulp down one cup after another, forcing ourselves to work at a frenetic pace until we arrive home at night as limp as a used coffee filter. Exercise—we just don't have the energy. Yet studies show that thirty minutes of aerobic exercise a day gives your body the vigor to cope with job stress. If you don't have the energy to go thirty minutes, start with twenty or ten. Dust off that exercise bike, slip into that jogging suit, and widen the margins of your life.

May I find the strength to overcome my own inertia.

"The only thing we can do for eight hours a day, day after day, is work."
—William Faulkner

Faulkner sadly underestimated the workaholic's capacity to put in ten to twelve hours a day, six days a week. Of course, many of us say that we love what we do for a living—our work is our play. Our attitude seems to be "Thank goodness it's Monday." But therein lies our problem. We throw ourselves into our jobs with such enthusiasm, energy, and abandon that we lose all sense of perspective, all sense of self-worth outside of work.

Reflections:

According to Parkinson's law, work expands to fill the time allotted to it. If you want to cut back on your overtime, make a point of scheduling other activities on your daily calendar. Book a game of tennis or racquetball with someone, join a golf foursome, or make a regular date to go walking with a friend. By committing to someone else, you increase your chances of following through on your plans.

I'm going to schedule some fun with a friend today.

OCTOBER 17

"Leisure, rather than work, provides the purest definition of self."

—Aristotle

Asked if he or she had a good time on vacation, a workaholic is apt to reduce the entire experience to a string of numbers, as if fun could be measured to the third decimal point. "We averaged 386.5 miles a day . . . I got 21.2 miles to the gallon . . . shot 46 on the back nine . . . caught twelve crappies and three muskies the first day . . . temperature never dropped below 82 degree." A fixation with numbers leads to a frenetic effort to squeeze more and more into each day so that, instead of relaxing, we return home from vacation in need of a rest.

Relaxation.:

Imagine what it would be like to describe your next vacation in terms like these: "I left my watch at home . . . awakened whenever I felt like it . . . took a morning walk and an afternoon swim, relaxed with a book, and never once wore a pair of socks." In planning your next vacation, pick a secluded spot, away from the bright lights and traffic, a place where the only timepiece is the sun and the tempo is set by the rhythm of the surf, a place where you can walk to the sandy beaches, get a tan, and skip stones across the waves, oblivious to time.

I can read the travel folders now and become an armchair traveler.

"He that hath wife and children, hath given hostages to fortune."
—Francis Bacon

As a workaholic, you have probably shared the rewards of your success with your family. The symbols of your affection are everywhere to be seen: new cars in the garage, furs hanging in the hallway closet, fine furniture, stereos, computer, original art throughout the home, and mementos of exotic vacations. The one thing you may not have given your family is yourself. Even when you are physically present, and appear to be listening, your mind may be at the office. You're unable to relax and enjoy quality time with your family.

Reflections:

Of all the gifts you could lavish on the members of your family, none is as precious in their eyes as the gift of yourself. They know you too well to be fooled when you feign attention. They may not be able to understand the technical complexities of the problems that distract you, but they can empathize with how you feel. Open up and share those feelings so they can relate to you on that level. At the same time, be prepared to listen to where they're at— listen with your whole being.

My family is my greatest blessing.

"You only live once—but if you work it right, once is enough."
—Joe E. Lewis

How long has it been since you wandered leisurely through an art gallery or museum, listening intently to the guide, studying the exhibits, losing yourself in time? When was the last time you attended the symphony or opera and gave yourself over in reverie to the music? Do you recall the last time you went to the theater or a ball game without a client being present? Can you enjoy a game of poker, bridge, or gin rummy without playing for high stakes? Our pastimes reveal a lot about our attitude toward leisure.

Reflections:

To a hyperactive workaholic, many pastimes seem too time consuming, slow-paced, and noncompetitive. We're so exhausted after work that we can't seem to muster the energy necessary to concentrate for any length of time. As soon as the theater lights dim, our eyes close, and we nod off. Afterward, we read the program to find out what we missed. Our relaxation time is edited, condensed, and squeezed between the margins of a playbill.

This week, instead of entertaining a client, I'm going to entertain myself.

"Few people do business well who do nothing else."

—Lord Chesterfield

In the mid-seventeenth century, Europeans incarcerated the indigent and unemployed along with the insane. The one thing these three groups had in common was idleness, a cardinal sin in the emerging mercantile world. Among the Seven Deadly Sins, sloth was considered the worst by the industrious burghers and tradespeople. In the medieval view, idleness was the root of all vice and anyone who could not or would not work was "crazy." Many of these same attitudes persist today, due to confusion between laziness and leisure.

Reflections:

Do you feel "guilty" when you cut back on your work load? If so, it's important to recognize the difference between laziness and leisure. Kierkegaard said laziness is a "despairing refusal to be oneself" and use all of one's God-given talents. Leisure is not laziness. It is the serene and quiet contemplation of unfathomable mysteries of creation. It is the active acceptance of our Higher Power's plan for our life. It is a form of prayer and celebration.

I'm going to offer up my leisure time as a form of prayer.

*"It's not the greatness of a man's means
that makes him independent so much as
the smallness of his wants."*
—William Cobbet

What do you suppose all these companies have in common?—AMR Corporation, American President, Inc., CSX Corporation, XTRA Corporation, USX Corporation. Not Sure? Here's a clue: their daily performance affects decisions in hundreds of firms like yours, most of which have never done business with them. Still in doubt? You're not alone. The fact is few of us can identify these or other companies that comprise the Dow Jones Industrial Average. Yet we accept as gospel these and other "key indicators" without questioning their relevance to our lives.

Reflections:

When your peace of mind is linked to factors beyond your control, your emotional stock can go through wild gyrations over events that need not concern you. To maintain your equilibrium, focus on the here and now and ask yourself how things are going. Chances are, you have a lot to be bullish about.

When I take stock of my whole situation, I have a lot to be thankful for.

"Only a person who can live with himself can enjoy the gift of leisure."
—Henry Greber

Vacations can be very stressful times for a workaholic. Our biorhythms, attuned to the exciting, fast pace of our businesses, are out of sync with the slower rhythm of our surroundings. We're impatient with waiters who operate on "island time" and with natives who tell us to "hang loose." Our overstimulated psyches are bored with "doing nothing" and discomforted by the lack of structure and the free time to just be ourselves. We engage in rotary thinking in which our minds race from the past through the present to the future and back again, going over our business problems again and again.

Reflections:

The harder you work on the job, the greater you need to get away from it all. You need time to restore yourself and reflect on what you want out of life, and what you hope to give back. It can take three or four days to wind down and become present to the moment, but when your thoughts become clear you'll have a much better idea of where you're at and where you're headed.

I'm not going to bring a single business book on vacation.

"The best intelligence test is what we do with our leisure."

—Laurence J. Peter

If you travel extensively on business, as many workaholics do, you look forward to time at home to relax and enjoy the company of family and friends. The thought of spending your vacation living out of a suitcase, jumping on and off tour buses, climbing over antiquities, or roughing it at a cabin may not be appealing. But if you vacation close to home—and the office—the danger is that you will reach for the phone "just to check in" with your secretary and soon find yourself back at your desk!

Reflections:

The majority of the "frequent flyer" miles earned have never been redeemed! The airlines are counting on the fact that you will never get around to taking your vacation. Maybe you can't afford a solid two-week stretch away from the office, but your travel agent can help you plan a seven-day, six-night trip. If that isn't feasible, plan a combination business-and-pleasure trip. And, if that isn't possible, plan a series of long weekends at resorts within one day's drive of your home.

I'm going to put some careful planning and research into my next vacation.

OCTOBER 24

*"The happiness of a man in this life
does not consist in the absence, but in
the mastery of his passions."*
—Lord Alfred Tennyson

Could you survive without your character flaws,
those strong personality traits that have played such
a large part in defining your workaholic behavior?
Bad habits develop when our workaholic behavior
receives positive reinforcement. Ask yourself what
payback do you get when you overwork yourself.
Chances are, your reward is the respect and concern
of others for your well-being. You enjoy the role of
sainted martyr, and—just in case no one notices—
you are quick to complain about how hard you
work, especially to your spouse.

Reflections:

All of us need the strong support of family and
friends to cope with stress. But if your complaining
becomes chronic, their sympathy may become resentment. They may feel used and abused because
they can do nothing about your workload. The next
time you're tempted to complain about work, share
some good news about your company instead. You
may be surprised at how attentive your listeners become.

*There's no sense complaining about work if I'm not
willing to do something about it.*

OCTOBER 25

"Sleep is sweet to the laboring man, whether he eats little or much, but the rich man's abundance allows him no sleep."

—Ecclesiastes 5:11

Unlike many animals, we do not spend our days hunting, grazing, foraging, or scavenging for food. The food we need for sustenance is abundant and accessible, and our metabolic system operates efficiently on light meals composed of readily available foods. We're free to spend much of our days pursuing spiritual rather than bodily needs.

Reflections:

Anything more than we need to sustain ourselves conditions us to think that we need more. And the more we need, the more we want from society and nature. We work harder longer and more diligently, surrounding ourselves with abundance, spreading our table lavishly to satiate our desires, filling our bank accounts, stuffing our closets with clothes. We can actually make more money at a weekend garage sale than many Third World families earn in a year.

Give us this day our daily bread.

"Enough is a feast."

—Irish proverb

For a workaholic, one of the most efficacious forms of prayer is fasting. Mentioned in Scripture seventy-five times, fasting is a form of penance and self-discipline that helps control our impulsiveness and need for instant gratification. It changes us, rather than our circumstances; we can immediately feel its effect on our lives. We lose up to two pounds a day and purge our bodies of toxins. Fasting also creates a heightened state of awareness and a sense of calm detachment. In fact, research shows fasting lowers the metabolic rate as much as 22 percent. Yet people on a fast feel highly energized.

Reflections:

Before fasting, get your doctor's approval. Then pick twenty-four hours in which you abstain from all foods and liquids, except water. Don't tell others what you are doing. Offer up your fast in silent prayer. As the day progresses, you'll appreciate the extra hour and a half you have to yourself because you're not eating. And at the end of the day you'll feel clear-headed, composed, and better able to make decisions.

I'm going to fast for twenty-four hours.

*"Good habits are as easy to form as bad
ones."*

—Tim McCarver

Our memory forms holographic three-dimensional images, rather than flat two-dimensional pictures of our past, with each experience recorded at more than one site in the brain. Like a hologram, our memories can be reduced to a mere fraction of their original size, but the image remains—it is not as bright, but it's still there. If you want to erase a memory or habit of thought, you have to change all your mental associations with that activity.

Reflections:

A habit can be replaced by another habit in about six weeks of persistent effort. It doesn't happen overnight, but it can be achieved over time through constant practice. If you're trying to change your workaholic behavior, develop another habit. One workaholic began cooking the family meals so he would have to be home by 6:00 p.m. each night. It not only forced him to set a firm quitting time, but he also found that cooking was a creative and relaxing escape from the cares of the office.

I'm going to take a three-dimensional approach to fun: relaxation, meditation, and celebration.

OCTOBER 28

"The family is the nucleus of civilization."

—Will and Ariel Durant

"Not now—can't you see that I'm busy?" . . . "Wait until I get my work done." . . . "Sorry, son, but this report is due tomorrow." Which of us hasn't said something like this when our work interfered with a family situation? Somehow work always wins out because it is our job—as if being a spouse and a parent weren't important jobs. Eventually, it's just understood by the rest of the family that things such as dance recitals and ball games are not as important as your paperwork. At least that's the message they get from all those memos you write at night.

Reflections:

Spouse and parent. When you think about it, they're the two most important jobs you have. But there is no one to supervise your performance, no formal training program, and no written job description. It's up to you to decide what you'll put into those jobs. No success in life can compensate for failure in the home.

I'm going to write my job description for spouse and parent.

*"The tragedy of life is what dies inside
a man while he lives."*
—Albert Schweitzer

If you are compulsive about your work, there is
a good chance you are compulsive about other activities such as chain-smoking, coffee drinking, drugs,
or alcohol. Substance abuse is another way to alter
your mood and cope with the adrenalin high you
get from work. It's a misguided attempt at gaining
control over your addiction to stress. Of course, it
fails to alleviate your anxiety and depression for
long, and eventually aggravates the very problems
you were trying to remedy. But by then you're too
strung out to notice.

Reflections:

Do you smoke? Do you drink more than three
cups of coffee a day? Do you need sleeping pills or
tranquilizers to sleep at night? Do you drink more
than two pints of beer a day, or half a bottle of wine,
or three and a half measures of alcohol? If so, work
is not your only compulsion, and if you continue to
abuse yourself this way the only thing you will have
left in the end is your ambition.

*Reliance on stimulants and depressants is a sure
sign that my ambition is all consuming.*

> *"It was not Christ's intention to reject or despise fasting ... it was his intention to restore fasting."*
> —Martin Luther

The simple life begins with a simple diet because food, after all, sustains life. Our attitude toward food subtly shapes our attitude toward all possessions, all things that we take unto ourselves. Every meal is a temptation to eat more than we need, to ask for seconds, to add more spices, consume more wine, and add a rich dessert. Every meal is an occasion to satiate our desires, not just our needs, and so dull our senses that we no longer appreciate simple things.

Reflections:

We become what we eat. If we indulge in rich, gourmet meals, our extravagance doesn't end when we push away from the table. We seek more and more self-gratification, and our lives become as complex as the recipes we consume. The simple life has a simple diet, one low in cholesterol, calories, sweets, and spices.

I'm going to eliminate sweet and salty snacks from my diet.

OCTOBER 31

"Our very business in life is not to get ahead of others but to get ahead of ourselves."

—Thomas L. Manson

In some parts of the country, the number of autos is growing at a faster rate than the human population. For millions of commuters, rush-hour traffic is an obstacle course that can take a half hour or longer to complete. That means we spend approximately two years of our lives in gridlock, car windows rolled up, engines roaring, communicating with each other by bumper sticker only.

Reflections:

The next time you're stuck in traffic take a closer look at the bumper stickers, scriptures for our times: "I'd rather be fishing," "I owe, I owe, it's off to work I go," "Work is a four-letter word." Bumper stickers are colorful shorthand expressions of our values, our philosophy. If you had to express your own philosophy about work in a ten-word bumper sticker, what would it say?

Success is a direction, not a destination.

NOVEMBER

Self-Actualization

Through prayer and meditation, we can improve our contact with our Higher Power, and develop a clearer idea of how our gifts in life can be used to fulfill our destiny. In the solitude and silence of meditation, we find the strength we need to take one day at a time and the serenity to let go and let our Higher Power take control of our lives. We feel more at peace in our business affairs and experience a deep sense of gratitude for the way our Higher Power has deigned to use our talents to the fullest. We are at peace with ourselves.

NOVEMBER 1

"Our strength is often composed of the weaknesses we're damned if we're going to show."

—Mignon McLaughlin

Most workaholics struggle with the issue of self-esteem. One measure of self-esteem is the willingness to be honest with yourself and recognize both your strengths and weaknesses. Of course, knowing your strengths allows you to maximize opportunities that call for your skills. But by the same token, knowing your weaknesses means you can compensate for them or avoid situations in which your weaknesses are apparent.

Reflections:

To be a truly effective executive, you must lead from strength and conceal your weaknesses. If you are conscious of your shortcomings, you can surround yourself with people who have compensating skills. By filling in your gaps, these staff members strengthen your management position. They feel as if they're making a meaningful contribution and are not threatened by head-to-head competition with you. They feel good about themselves and are energized by working for you because you bring out the best in them—and the best in yourself.

I'm at my best when I bring out the best in others.

NOVEMBER 2

"Maturity consists of no longer being taken in by oneself."
—Kajetan von Schlaggenberg

As the originator of the business conglomerate, Royal Little built Textron into a multibillion-dollar corporation and later created another immensely successful company called Narragansett Capital. Yet this highly respected member of the Business Hall of Fame summed up his career in a book entitled *How to Lose a Hundred Million Dollars and Other Valuable Advice*. In Little's view, you must be willing to admit your mistakes so that you can learn from them. You must be honest with yourself.

Reflections:

We workaholics have trouble being honest with ourselves. We take on jobs that are outside our field of expertise, we accept an unrealistic work load, and we commit to deadlines we can't meet. When things go wrong, we blame it on circumstances instead of recognizing the error of our ways. As Thomas Jefferson noted, honesty is the first chapter in the book of wisdom.

I'm going to accept my own limitations.

"The most elusive knowledge of all is self-knowledge."
—Mirra Komarovsky

All of us want to make our mark in the business world. The need for recognition is a dominant theme in a workaholic's life because the approval of others helps compensate for our own inner doubts. To earn the esteem of our co-workers, we willingly pay a steep price—the physical, mental, and emotional toll of a 70-hour work week. In effect, we choose the image of success over the reality of a diminished personal life.

Reflections:

Despite the appearance of success, many of us do not feel successful. We feel cheated and angry because, no matter how hard we work, we cannot feel fulfilled by the recognition of others. The promotions and awards don't satisfy us because they honor our public personas rather than our true selves. We exchange self-respect for status, and our health for wealth, because—as one workaholic put it—"Glory is fleeting, but obscurity is forever." As long as our self-esteem depends on what others think of us, we will feel unfilled and restless.

If I try to please everyone, the last person I'll satisfy is myself.

"There is dignity in work only when it is work freely accepted."
— Albert Camus

Workaholism is so widespread that it is easy to rationalize and say to yourself, "I'm not the only one working overtime—everyone's doing it." You certainly can find support for that view in the facts and figures on work load stress levels in the aftermath of the restructuring of corporate America. But there is small comfort to be derived from counting yourself among the working wounded. When your job starts to affect your mental, physical, and emotional well-being, citing economic statistics is simply an attempt to intellectualize an intensely personal problem. Have enough self-respect to do something about your job.

Reflections:

Each of us has a different capacity for work. Your intellect, musculature, and nervous system set an upper limit to the amount of work you can handle comfortably. Regardless of what the economists say about the productivity of the U.S. worker, you know how hard you're working, and you know whether or not you're feeling stressed out. Recovery from workaholism begins when you accept the fact that you're only human.

No one can make me work overtime without my permission.

> *"Rule of survival: Pack your own para-chute."*
>
> —T. L. Hakala

There is such a thing as a workaholic company in which the senior executives expect, and demand ceaseless effort. Often the result of a company crisis, such as a major new competitor, this sort of systemic workaholism spreads through the company like a virus. Chronic understaffing, high turnover, endless meetings, obsolete job descriptions, and a patchwork quilt organization chart are just some of the symptoms. The inefficiencies inherent in the system almost oblige you to work overtime.

Reflections:

If you're employed by a workaholic company and choose to remain, there are a number of things you can do to insulate yourself against the excessive stress. Consider joining a car pool so that your arrival and departure times are fixed. Schedule several lunches a week with friends who work for another company. Get an unlisted phone number or answering machine so you can't be disturbed at night and on weekends. Avoid country clubs, sports clubs, and volunteer groups that are somehow connected to work.

My private life belongs to me. What I do after hours is my business.

"When you're through changing, you're through."

—Bruce Barton

Most workaholics think they are highly disciplined people simply because they work so hard. Actually, our workaholism is not a sign of discipline, but of its opposite trait, compulsion—behavior without choice. We have allowed our jobs to intrude into every area of our lives because we lack the discipline necessary to establish clearly defined boundaries for business and personal activities. For the better part of our lives, we have allowed others to set our boundaries for us. Without a strong sense of self-worth, we don't know when to say no.

Reflections:

No matter how ingrained your workaholism is, you can change for the better, starting today. It can be as simple as deciding the hour at which you will arrive and leave the office each day. It could be setting a firm time and place for daily meditation, or an hour for exercise. Whatever it is, take that first step today. Establishing a routine that separates your business and personal life is the sign of true discipline and a measure of your sense of self-worth.

Where my personal life is concerned, I have to learn to say yes.

"He who does his work like a machine grows a heart like a machine, and he who carries the heart of a machine in his breast loses his simplicity."

—Tzu-Gung

One way of coping with a heavy work load is to adopt a stoic attitude: "The difficult we do immediately; the impossible takes a little longer; miracles by appointment only." But by deadening yourself to the pain of a punishing work load, you anesthetize all your feelings, and that includes the feeling of exhilaration and satisfaction at having done a job well. With the passage of time, you require more and more effort to feel satisfied with what you have achieved. You are numb to success, and your sense of self is diminished.

Reflections:

Losing contact with your own feelings is an eerie sensation. You sense that you are on the outside looking in, observing yourself going through the motions. Action becomes an escape from the emptiness you feel, so you step up the tempo of your work until eventually sheer exhaustion forces you to stop. You may be on the fast track, but you're running on empty. Does it have to reach that point before you get in touch with your feelings?

Today, I'm going to perform a real miracle and leave the office at 5:00 P.M.

*"The great art of life is sensation, to feel
that we exist, even in pain."*
—Lord Byron

True workaholics won't let anything stand in
the way of success, not even their feelings. They
submerge themselves in the role of a cool, unflapp-
able professional and hide their emotions behind a
mask of success. Like a method actor who has mem-
orized every pose, they play their part to perfection,
but without a strong show of emotion. Feelings
might put them in touch with their true self and
with vulnerabilities they do not want to admit.

Reflections:

We have such a strong need to appear perfect
that we sublimate any emotion that might threaten
our self-control. In disowning our emotions, we disown ourselves and experience the strange sensation
of standing in the wings, watching ourselves perform, spectators in our own lives. Our detachment
is felt by those around us who sense that we're "lost
in thought." Life becomes a vicarious experience.
We need to get in touch with our own true feelings
by taking our emotional inventory. Spend a few moments now reviewing your journal entries, and ask
yourself how it feels to relive the experiences.

*My life is a script without stage directions. It's up
to me to interpret the part.*

NOVEMBER 9

"Failure is success if we learn from it."
—Malcolm S. Forbes

As a hard-charging, action-oriented workaholic, you may not be pursuing success so much as fleeing from emotions you're not ready to face. Frenetic activity is one way of releasing the tension that accumulates from pent-up feelings. The emotion driving many workaholics is the fear of failure. It's difficult to admit to ourselves, but fear is often present, just below the surface, a fault line in our self-confidence, undermining our decisions, causing us to quake, pursue conflicting objectives, and above all work harder.

Reflections:

Naming an emotion and dealing with it are two different things. Fear of failure is difficult to face as long as you see things as all or nothing, black and white. The truth is, there is no such thing as total, unconditional failure. In fact, there is no such thing as failure in the eyes of many successful people. Sure, they have setbacks, just like the rest of us, but rather than see them as failures, they see them as learning experiences or stepping-stones to success. You can learn more from your failures than you can from success.

As long as I am willing to try, I cannot fail.

"All I have to give you is my good name.
Pass it on."

—Rand V. Araskog

Behind many great achievers, there is another great success, a mentor or role model who trained and inspired them. The role model may be a figure of history, a parent, a friend, or a boss. Rand Araskog, of ITT, chose his father as his role model. John Sculley, of Apple Computer, patterned himself after Don Kendall, president of Pepsico when Sculley worked there. And Charles Brown of AT&T studied under John DeButts. When asked, "What have been the major influences in helping you become an executive?" 47.6 percent of the CEOs named a manager early in their career who acted as a model.

Reflections:

Do you have a role model, someone you respect? To some extent, your success in business hinges on your willingness to model your performance on that of a superior. If you're constantly challenging superiors and insisting on the freedom to do things your way, you may lose out to someone else who has a mentor helping to advance his or her career. Choose a role model you admire rather than one you may have to compete against.

Before I can become a leader, I must learn to be a follower.

"The essential factor that lifts one man above his fellows in terms of achievement and success is his capacity for greater self-discipline."

—Ray Kroc

As the founder of McDonald's, Ray Kroc demonstrated the importance of discipline by instituting a training program and operating system that made his fast food restaurants models of efficiency. We tend to think of "discipline" as a punishing adherence to a set of rules or procedures. But in reality "self-disciplined" people are free to enjoy the fruits of self-mastery: success, leisure, and the joy that comes from knowing we have done our best.

Reflections:

Self-mastery begins with self-respect, accepting your own strengths and weaknesses. Truly self-disciplined people know when to work and when to rest. They have well-defined value systems or rules of conduct that guide their every action, and their motivation is to be the best that they can be in all phases of their lives. Why not make a commitment today to take charge of every aspect of your life? Write it down so you can look back on it for inspiration when you feel pressured to compromise.

Grant me the self-discipline to control the urge to work on my days off.

NOVEMBER 12

"Reality is larger than life."
                                        —Bob Larrañaga

Each of us is the center of our own universe. As we experience reality, everything revolves around us; so naturally we expect to be the center of attention, the star. When things don't go our way—for example, if we don't get a promotion or raise—we're surprised and disappointed. It's not supposed to happen this way. Suddenly our self-centeredness becomes self-pity. We blame it on bad luck, exaggerate the difficulties we faced, and say we did the best we could under the circumstances.

Reflections:

If you find yourself focusing on the difficulties you face, you may be settling for sympathy instead of success. Sympathy has a certain amount in common with success: we are the center of attention and our efforts are admired. But once we cast ourselves in the "martyr" role, our work seems to take on a redemptive quality, and the very thought of relaxing bothers our conscience. We become the center of a very small universe circumscribed by our work.

True success can only be achieved when I recognize that I am not the center of the universe.

> *"Everybody experiences far more than he understands. Yet it is experience, rather than understanding, that influences behavior."*
> —Marshall McLuhan

There is no such thing as 20–20 hindsight. Our vision of the past is distorted by our natural tendency to organize things into a cohesive, logical pattern that makes sense. When viewed in this manner, the events take on a certain inevitability and the outcome seems so obvious, in retrospect, that we feel foolish for not knowing that penny stock would quintuple, the boss's deadline was unrealistic, and our best client was talking to a competitor. We berate ourselves needlessly.

Reflections:

Second-guessing ourselves this way undermines our self-respect. The fact of the matter is that life doesn't always make sense. The outcome is often in doubt and frequently settled at the last moment by the complex interplay of scarcely recognized and little understood forces. When you oversimplify what happened, you do yourself an injustice, and you make it difficult to analyze what really occurred so that you can learn from the past.

In analyzing my own performance, I'll give myself benefit of the doubt.

> "A committee is twelve men doing the
> work of five."
>
> —John F. Kennedy

We are all somewhat egocentric and tend to take
more credit for a joint project than others might
grant us. When we sense that we are not getting the
credit we "deserve," we think that others are taking
advantage of us and we become aggressive. It never
occurs to us that our view of reality is not shared by
the others, and that in their eyes we are laying claim
to their contributions. This cause of office politics is
extremely wide-spread, though seldom confronted
directly, because most projects result in team credit
rather than individual credit.

Reflections:

Of course, at times others try to take more credit
than is due. But to an aggressive workaholic even
well-meaning co-workers can appear to be overreaching. In our egocentricity, we dwell on our own
ideas and filter out what others say. We are more
receptive to our own thoughts because they fit within our value system. And, we are more familiar with
our efforts than those of our co-workers. (For example, we might not know if they had worked at night
on the project.) As a result, we emphasize our own
role on a project and deemphasize that of others.

I'm going to make an extra effort to be a team player.

NOVEMBER 15

"We live in the midst of alarms; anxiety beclouds the future; we expect some new disaster with each newspaper we read."
—Abraham Lincoln

The morning paper arrives with news of the latest armed conflict, another presidential appointment, a disaster in some Third World country, and the outbreak of a flu epidemic. But, nowhere, not once on any single pages does your name appear, anywhere. Congratulations, your problems didn't make the headlines again! Sure, they may seem overwhelming at times, but when viewed in the larger context most personal problems are manageable, provided we don't lapse into self-pity.

Reflections:

Short of pain, self-pity is the most tiring experience to which we can subject ourselves. When we focus on our problems and exaggerate them, we weigh ourselves down emotionally and psychologically. We begin to think of ourselves as martyrs, tragic heroes. More often than not, we don't have a problem; we have a pattern—a pattern of thinking that is self-defeating. If you want to break the pattern, take a closer look at the headlines in today's newspaper and ask yourself if you would change places with any of those people.

If it isn't life threatening, it isn't a problem.

NOVEMBER 16

"The closest to perfection a person ever comes is when he fills out a job application from."
—Stanley J. Randall

Have you ever exaggerated on a résumé or in a job interview? Thirty percent of all job applicants do, according to Robert Half and Associates, a personnel recruitment firm. Each of us has a desire to appear perfect to others. The trouble with establishing such impossible standards is that it sets us up to fail again and again. Unchecked, perfectionism leads to self-criticism, anxiety, depression, and withdrawal. In the end, every perfectionist is a guaranteed loser.

Reflections:

Workaholics strive to appear perfect at all costs. But once we start exaggerating to others about our performance, we become entrapped in our own web of deceit. Better not to exaggerate in the first place. An honest, humble assessment of our strengths and weaknesses is a prerequisite to overcoming our compulsion to work.

Everyone makes mistakes, but mistakes only become errors when one fails to acknowledge them.

"Do not tell me how hard you work, tell me how much you get done."
— James J. Ling

In a study conducted by a major corporation, 80 percent of the employees said they did an above-average job. Of course, these results are statistically impossible (at best, only 50 percent are above average), but they help explain why many people feel that their company doesn't give them the credit they deserve. Simply put, it's difficult to be objective about our own performance and easy to rationalize any shortcomings we might have. Workaholics are especially prone to these types of feelings, because we equate extra effort with superior performance

Reflections:

There's one sure way to make certain you get the credit you deserve, and that's to follow the lead of Ed Koch, former mayor of New York, who constantly asked, "How am I doing?" But when you ask the question, be prepared to hear the truth. The hard reality is that management isn't interested in how hard we worked "under the circumstances." It expects us to rise above the circumstances. We're paid for results, not effort.

One thing I have to work harder on is a realistic assessment of my work.

NOVEMBER 18

"Becoming less perfect takes practice."
—Colette Dowling

Once your self-worth is linked to some arbitrary standard, you are bound to be riven by feelings of doubt and inadequacy. If, for example, your standard is the opinion of your boss, you're never sure how you're doing, because your boss (like most people) is constantly changing his or her mind. In fact, you are seldom on your boss's mind; your boss is too busy wondering about his or her own self-worth to give any thought to yours! Yet if your standard of self-worth is some personal idea of perfection, you're also guaranteed to feel inadequate, because you will always fall short of perfection.

Reflections:

The toughest boss you'll ever work for is yourself. You scrutinize every decision, every action, and every mistake you make. You compare yourself to some impossible standard and belittle your performance when you fall short. When was the last time you gave yourself credit for doing a good job—not a "perfect job"—but a good one? When was the last time you congratulated yourself for remaining calm in a crisis? For running a smooth meeting? For defusing an irate customer? For learning from a mistake? Make a habit of giving yourself credit just for being you.

As my own boss, I'm going to give myself time off.

> *"The fundamental motive of human be-*
> *havior is not self-preservation, but the*
> *preservation of the symbolic self, or self-*
> *concept."*
>
> —S. I. Hayakawa

The goal of all human activity, according to se-manticist S. I. Hayakawa, is to have the self-image outlive the true self—a bid for immortality. We want to live on in our offspring and in the ideas we pass on to them, to live in the memories of others, and to survive in the possessions we leave behind. For many executives, the bid for immortality centers around work. We want to "make a name" for our-selves in business, earn a big promotion, a new title, a larger office, and a staff. Eventually, we hope to see our name on the door and possibly across the panel of a truck or the side of a building.

Reflections:

The goal of every workaholic is to have chiseled on his or her tombstone, "Off to another meeting." We bury ourselves in work in the hope of building a lasting monument to our success. Unfortunately, as a claim on immortality, a business does not serve very well. Less than 30 percent of all businesses sur-vive into the third generation. Too late, the worka-holic discovers he or she has built a mausoleum instead of a monument.

Grant me the faith I need to live one day at a time in the eternal now.

"One nice thing about egotists: They don't talk about other people."
—Lucille S. Harper

A 1974 study supervised by Lawrence Scherwitz of the University of Wisconsin, revealed that students who showed the Type A (hard-driving behavior pattern) used first-person pronouns frequently, and when they did, their blood pressure shot up. This led to another study among 150 men admitted to the hospital for angiograms. Here again, the researchers saw that Type A men used frequent self-references, had more extensively blocked arteries, and more second heart attacks. Psychologist Lynda Powell, while at Stanford, also observed from interviews that one of the highest predictors of a second heart attack was the number of personal references men used in answering the question "About what do you feel insecure?"

Reflections:

Self-centeredness is a problem we all confront, even in prayer. Instead of lifting our minds and hearts to a Higher Power, we concentrate on ourselves and our needs. Why not spend a few moments today praying for someone you know who is in need? Then call that person and offer to be of help; sometimes all it takes is an encouraging word. Give of yourself.

"He who confers benefits will be amply enriched, and he who refuses others will himself be refused." (Proverbs 11:25).

"Most people are other people. Their thoughts are someone else's opinions, their lives a mimicry, their passions a quotation."

—DeProfundis

The business journals devote their covers and glossy photo spreads to corporate titans, larger-than-life figures whose bold exploits somehow diminish our own achievements on a weekly basis. We may adopt their ideas, echo their statements, and pattern our behavior after theirs, without ever knowing whether they are truly successful at the business of life. We can only guess at the personal price they've paid for their success and ask ourselves whether it is worth it.

Reflections:

Why is it so much easier to count someone else's blessings? How often have you said to yourself, "I'd give anything to be in his place?" At times like this it might help to write in your daily journal a list of all your blessings. Then imagine for a moment how you'd feel if you lost all of them, and—more importantly—how elated you would be if they were suddenly restored. When you think about it, there are a lot of people who would give anything to be in your place.

Ultimately, all philosophy is biography. My daily journals are the best indicator of my self-respect.

NOVEMBER 22

> *"You know things aren't going well at work when your adjustable chair has been adjusted to fit someone else."*
> —Garrison Keillor

The perquisites of office are the most tangible signs of our role in the corporate caste system. According to one biographer of Henry Ford II, Lee Iacocca's abuse of the perk system led to his downfall: he didn't know his role. Role ambiguity is a major problem in corporations and a real stressor for workaholics who are born rebels. If you haven't had a scheduled raise, if there are rumors of cutbacks, and if you've been surprised by a change that affects you, you have to cope. For many of us, that means smoking, overeating, drinking, or spending—all of which increase stress, ultimately.

Reflections:

If you can't change the situation, change your attitude. Since the problem is role ambiguity, self-affirmation is important. You need the support of close friends and the positive reinforcement you get in meditation. Tell yourself this situation will pass. See yourself winning. Look upon this challenge as a way to grow. Get some audio cassette tapes on positive mental attitude, and listen to them while you walk or jog.

I've given my best to the company, and that's all it can expect.

"Dreams are the touchstones of our character."

—Henry David Thoreau

Do you dream of "success unexpected in common hours?" When your self-esteem is based solely on what you achieve, it's possible to love your work more than you love yourself. Intellectual work is especially seductive because there are no limits to what you can achieve in your imagination: you can dream impossible dreams while ignoring the real physical and emotional signs that you've reached your limits. In losing yourself in your work, you lose touch with your true feelings and fall in love with the image of success.

Reflections:

Our sense of self derives in part from our bodily feelings. Without those feelings, we have no clear idea of our limits. We overcommit ourselves and set unrealistic, grandiose goals. We tell ourselves we don't need seven hours' sleep, that we're quick studies, that we thrive on pressure. Yet we remain unfulfilled because our spirit is impoverished by the loss of feelings we have disowned. The truly successful have a strong sense of self-worth that allows them to acknowledge their limitations and use them to channel their energies in productive ways.

I'm going to make a list of my greatest strengths and weaknesses.

NOVEMBER 24

*"Every man has three characters—that
which he exhibits, that which he has,
and that which he thinks he has."*
—Alphonse Karr

One of the best ways to get in touch with who
you are is by writing your family history. You are,
after all, a product of nature and nurture. The genes
you inherited determined your temperament and
talent, and the environment in which you were
raised helped shape your personality, value system,
and goals. Your first and most important role models
were your parents. Your siblings were your most important peers during the formative stages of your
life. To understand your family, and your role within it, is to better understand yourself.

Reflections:

Seek out the eldest members of your family,
with pencil, paper, and tape recorder in hand, and
ask them to outline the family tree. Then ask them
to describe what your ancestors were like: What
kind of work did they do? What hobbies did they
have? What sort of personalities were they? Ask to
see photos and other memorabilia so that you form
a vivid mental picture of events. Ask other members
of the family for their recollections, as well. Once
you have a clear idea of the family history, write it
down so that you can begin to see the influences that
shaped your life.

I'm going to get in touch with my roots.

"There is nothing permanent except change."

—Heraclitus

Cereal box heroes and baseball cards. Pez candy and Marvel comics, Crayola crayons and Cracker Jack prizes, Charles Atlas and Wilt the Stilt. Those were the days. Innocent days. But that was then and this is now: astro turf and super domes, designer jeans and tanning parlors, Big Macs and tofu. Now you squint at the financial pages through bifocals and scan the news for stories with a comic book ending. The hero wins. All is well in Metropolis. And, yes, Elvis is alive and was last seen shopping at Nutrition World.

Reflections:

Few things in life turn out exactly as we expect. We're forced to adjust our thinking to the reality of our times. But, the changes occur imperceptibly— one grain of sand falls in the hour glass at a time. We don't realize how much we've changed until later, much later. When you think about it, though, you've already proven you're up to handling whatever changes time has in store for you.

I respect time, but I respect myself more.

"Self-respect is the root of discipline: the sense of dignity grows with the ability to say no to oneself."
—Abraham J. Heschel

In *Where Have I Been*, Sid Caesar tells how workaholism led to alcoholism, which diluted his comic genius and in its place left a figure of pathos. At the peak of his career, Caesar's *Show of Shows* broadcast live for two hours weekly. But the pressure to make others laugh drove him into drunken rages. The network canceled his show, and he lost everything, except the strong support of a devoted wife. He was so far down he had to look up to see bottom. But—like a true workaholic—he kept on working in the small lounges.

Reflections:

Today a recovering alcoholic, Sid Caesar credits his sobriety to self-acceptance. At the low point in his life, he hit on a novel way to get back in touch with who he was. He tape-recorded conversations with himself and listened to how he really felt. The voice on the tape recorder cut through the boozy fog and convinced Sid Caesar that he needed professional help. Are you at a low point in your life? Why not try recording your thoughts on work? You may be surprised at the insights you gain.

I'm within earshot of feeling better about myself.

"A man can stand a lot as long as he can stand himself."

—Axel Munthe

The president of a fast-track company had assembled his key executives at a weekend retreat to discuss the company's future plans. When the maitre d' asked about who should sit where during lunch, the executive's response was simple and to the point: "Those that matter won't mind where they sit, and those that mind don't matter." Power, in an organization, is not a matter of position, but of inner strength.

Reflections:

All success is based on belief—belief in ourselves. If your self-worth is based on externals, sooner or later you will fail. But if your self-worth is based on the conviction that you are unique in some way and that your special gifts have marked you for a work in life that no one else can perform quite like you, then you are already a success.

I have to trust in my own ability to succeed.

*"Be yourself. Who else is better quali-
fied?"*
—Frank J. Giblin, II

How long has it been since you paged through
your family photo album? It can be an eye-opening
experience, especially for a workaholic. First, you
probably aren't in many of the photos because you
were too busy working. Second, the pictures you are
in were probably shot at family gatherings like wed-
dings, birthdays, and anniversaries so there are lots
of people in each scene. Are you hugging, touching,
kissing, laughing with other family members? Are
you relaxed or tense, animated or sullen? Do you
seem happy just being yourself among the people
who know you by your nickname instead of your
title?

Reflections:

Photo albums compress time into frozen images
of the high points of our lives: No one takes snap-
shots of the low points. Just the high points. How
long has it been since you had a picture-perfect day?
How old is the most recent photo of you smiling?
When you think about it, any day can be a perfect
day—it's all a matter of what you focus on.

I'm going to set my F-stop at "bright and cheerful."

*"A great success is to go through life as
a man who never gets used up."*
—Albert Schweitzer

The Fortune 1000 companies employ almost one of every three U.S. workers, and nearly every one of these corporate giants has been involved in a major restructuring in the past five years. Over one million professional and managerial jobs have disappeared as corporations down-sized, dismantled, and took on unprecedented debt. If your job hasn't been directly affected, you have at least felt threatened by economic forces beyond your control. In the back of your mind, you may have imagined the agony of the exit interview a thousand times, and in the process you have chipped away at your own self-esteem.

Reflections:

The events of the last few years, in which many talented and productive executives lost their jobs— through no fault of their own—underscore the fact that you cannot judge performance on results alone. You have to take into account individual effort and decide for yourself whether you've done your best for the company. If, in your mind, you've given your all, then you're a success.

Negative thinking is a sign of an overworked imagination.

"There is no such thing as pure pleasure; some anxiety always goes with it."
—Ovid

Which of us hasn't been forced at some point to choose between our family and our career? It may be as gutwrenching as choosing between a transfer to another city or staying put until your kids graduate. It may come down to whether you entertain an out-of-town client or attend your daughter's piano recital. It may be a choice between tennis with your boss or fishing with your son. No matter which choice you make, you feel torn, guilty—you can't please everyone—least of all yourself.

Reflections:

Those pangs of conscience may be a healthy sign that you've reordered your priorities in order to put your family first. Loved ones can play an important role in your recovery from workaholism. They can draw you out of yourself and distract you from your ever-present business problems. Whether applauding Beethoven's *Fifth* or enjoying a fish fry on the shore, you're present to the moment when you're present to your family.

My most important jobs are as spouse and parent.

DECEMBER

Spirituality

Having had a spiritual awakening as a result of these steps, we can share our blessings with others. By practicing these principles at work and by sharing them with co-workers struggling with workaholism, we can enter a new growth experience. Reflecting on where we have been, helps remind us how far we have come. At the same time, life's "unfinished business" provides us with new opportunities to use our talents in the service of others.

DECEMBER 1

"Always do right. This will surprise some people and astonish the rest."
—Mark Twain

Calling in sick when you're feeling well. Taking a two-hour lunch. Fudging on your expense account. Filching office supplies. The temptation is always there—to beat the system, settle a score with the company, address a wrong, especially if you've worked overtime and feel they "owe you one." But if you step over that invisible boundary you've said to yourself, once again, that there are no limits, anything goes, whatever it takes to win.

Reflections:

In all likelihood, the company won't notice minor transgressions. But if you compromise your standards in some small matter, it becomes easier to do so in larger ones. Without ever making a conscious ethical decision, you can find yourself in a conflict of interest that could jeopardize your career. It might be the revelation of confidential information in a job interview; or moonlighting for a competitor, or accepting gifts from suppliers. Whatever the case, no one steps over the line without smudging it first.

In keeping score, nothing counts more than integrity.

DECEMBER 2

*"The great law of culture: let each be-
come all that he was created capable of
being."*

—Thomas Carlyle

We sometimes take for granted the fact that
there is a spiritual dimension to our nature. But in
godless, totalitarian countries where religion is sup-
pressed, the human craving for the sublime finds
expression in other ways. In the Soviet Union, for
example, it is not uncommon to have 50,000 people
attend a poetry reading. Imagine a crowd as large as
those at many football games, sitting in rapt attention, listening to soul-stirring verses, and you begin
to appreciate how important it is to feed your spirit.

Reflections:

How fortunate we are to have access to the writing of history's greatest minds! Theologians, philos-
ophers, mystics, metaphysicians, and poets. How
lucky we are to be able to nourish our spirit with
the truly sublime, to be able to develop our own
informed point of view. This weekend, instead of
watching a ball game, why not spend some time in
spiritual reading?

*I have to nourish my soul as I would nourish my
body.*

DECEMBER 3

*"Work expands to fill the time available
for its completion."*
—Northcote Parkinson

The machine age began with the invention of
the clock sometime around the fourteenth century.
The impetus for measuring time came—not from la-
borers—but from monks concerned with faithfully
performing their religious duties. In fact, the word
clock derives from Middle Dutch term for the bell
that called monks to prayer. The day was originally
divided into prayer periods, rather than hours. Special devotionals were recited at first light (matins),
noon (meridies), and nightfall (compline), with the
number of chimes varying each time.

Reflections:

Ironically, the more preoccupied we became
with measuring time, the less concerned we grew
about its original purpose. The clocks on church
steeples were replaced by LED displays of time on
bank buildings, another reminder that time is money. In today's time-conscious society, there is never
enough time for quiet, prayerful reflection. We have
to make time to lift our spirits in prayer each day.

*My prayers will expand to fill the time allotted to
them.*

DECEMBER 4

*"There is as much difference between us
and ourselves as between us and others."*
—Michel Montaigne

Each of us plays many roles in the course of a
business day. At times, we discover who we are and
how we feel even as we speak, our unbidden words
revealing a side to ourselves that we didn't realize
existed until we hear it for the first time. We're surprised at the empathy we feel for an employee who
has just lost his or her job and taken a back a few
minutes later by the harshness that we display toward a vendor. We are capable of great changes, and
yet we are often surprised when they occur.

Reflections:

The reason we are surprised by our own behavior, social scientists say, is that our sense of self
changes very little overtime. We continue to see ourselves as we were in our prime and discount as ab-
errations any changes that don't fit our self-image.
Our hair may be streaked with silver and our waist-
line may be several matches wider, but when we
meet old acquaintances we're always surprised at
how much older they look. The one area of our lives
in which we can change for the better overtime is
our spirituality. Listen closely to what your thoughts
reveal about your spiritual growth and ask yourself
whether you're getting better or bitter.

I'm going to change for the better.

DECEMBER 5

"To pray is to change."
                                                    —Richard J. Foster

Prayer doesn't always change your circumstances, but it always changes you. So if you're having difficulty praying, it could be that you're not ready to change and are clinging to a form of self-defeating behavior. Imagine for a moment that you're listening to the voice of your Higher Power giving new direction and meaning to your life. What would you hear about your career so far? In what ways would your Higher Power praise your efforts? In what areas would you need to improve? Today is the first day of the rest of your life. You can start right now to change for the better.

Reflections:

Prayer can clear your mind of anxieties and worldly worries; free you of dependence on prestige, status symbols, and wealth; and it can open you to the possibility of a life-transforming experience. You don't have to be a philosopher or a biblical scholar to pray with power. Often the most powerful prayers are simply listening.

If I haven't heard from my Higher Power in a while, it's probably because I'm not listening.

DECEMBER 6

"Prayer does not change God, but it changes him who prays."
—Søren Kierkegaard

The Hopi Indians use the same word (*na wakana*) for "to will" and "to pray." In their culture, prayer is the turning of the will over to a Higher Power. In our culture, we have a tendency to wait until the last minute, when the situation is hopeless, before we turn to God. Then we surrender our problems, not our wills. We pray as though we're not quite sure our Higher Power is up to the job. When our prayers aren't answered immediately, we say, "Look, God, if you're not part of the solution, you're part of the problem!"

Reflections:

Taking matters into our own hands is second nature to workaholics. But sometimes the situation is beyond our grasp, and our only recourse is prayer. Our faith may not change the situation, but it can change us and the way we view things. When we turn our will over to a Higher Power, our business problems somehow seem small and easier to bear. In surrendering our need to control every situation, we come to realize that problems decrease as our faith increases.

God, I need you as a silent partner during these difficult days.

"Even after a bad harvest, there must be sowing."

—Lucius Seneca

Each spring for centuries, the Nile River flooded the surrounding farmlands with the runoff from the mountains to the south. Although their fields were flooded, the farmers waded into the floodplain to "cast their bread upon the waters," confident the seeds would take root in the fertile alluvial loam left by the receding waters. Within a few months, their faith was rewarded a hundredfold by a bountiful harvest. Like the Egyptian farmers, we risk when we take steps to deal with our workaholism.

Reflections:

Impatient for success, we often develop plans with unrealistic paybacks, and cross our fingers, hoping for success. This time, however, we must take a more patient, persevering approach because the problem we face is workaholism itself. Yes, there will be setbacks when we are swamped with work. But if we are resilient and confident in our ultimate success, we will be rewarded a hundredfold in due season.

Perseverance is another word for *success*.

DECEMBER 8

"Seek simplicity—and distrust it."
—Alfred North Whitehead

The paradox of simplicity is that everything seems simple until we come to understand it; only then do we realize how complex it is. You may understand what you have to do to simplify your job, but actually doing it, day by day, can be a complex matter involving an endless series of trade-offs. For every yes there must be a no; for every project you start another must stop; you can't have it all. Simplicity isn't easy. You have to work at it.

Reflections:

Simplicity is a form of surrender. It's the letting go of all our attachments, the things we place our trust in and that complicates our lives. We must become content with who we are in and of ourselves. This can only be achieved by spending time with ourselves in solitude. In meditation, we come to understand and accept our Higher Power's plan for our life. Solitude and meditation are the portals to a simpler life.

Grant me the simplicity of a trusting child.

DECEMBER 9

"That which God writes on His forehead,
thou wilt come to it."
—The Koran

Scheduled to speak in Philadelphia, Bishop Fulton J. Sheen decided to walk from his hotel to the town hall. However, he became lost and had to ask some boys for directions. One of them asked Sheen, "What are you going to do there?" "I'm giving a lecture," replied Sheen. "About what?" "On how to get to heaven. Would you care to come along?" "Are you kidding?" said the boy, "You don't even know how to get to Town Hall." Which of us hasn't felt lost at times and wondered whether we were following our Higher Power's plan for our lives?

Reflections:

The best clue as to what your Higher Power wants you to do with your life is the aptitudes and interests you've had since birth. Your genes are the blueprint for your life. If every career inventory test you've ever taken says you're a good accountant or lawyer, it's a safe bet your Higher Power doesn't expect you to be a missionary. By doing what you do best, and fulfilling your potential, you become a role model for others and a witness for your faith.

My actions at work are a silent witness to my faith.

DECEMBER 10

"I am part of all that I have met."
—Alfred Lord Tennyson

There is an Hasidic tale in which a rabbi asks his students, "How can we determine the hour of the dawn?" One student suggests, "When from a distance you can distinguish between a dog and a sheep?" "No," replies the rabbi. "When a man can distinguish between a fig tree and a grape vine?" asks a second student. "No," the rabbi says. "Please tell us the answer," says the students. "It is," he replies, "when you can look into the face of another and have enough light (in you) to recognize them as your brother or sister. Until then, it is night and darkness is still with us."

Reflections:

Your aggressive nature can lead you to think of co-workers as competitors to be beaten out for the next promotion or raise. You may label them as inferior; demean them with nicknames; question their competency or ethics. In the process, you lose sight of the real competition: yourself and your latent hostility. When was the last time that you congratulated a peer for a job well done?

When I feel hostile toward someone, I'll say a silent prayer for him or her.

"The finest fruit of serious learning should be the ability to speak the word 'God' without reserve or embarrassment."

—Anonymous

An olive tree in the garden of Gethsemane is over two thousand years old. Historians believe it dates back to the time of Jesus. Perhaps he leaned on it for support in a moment of anguish. The unknown gardener who planted that tree, watered its roots, and pruned its branches had no idea that people would enjoy the fruits of his or her labors and take shelter in its shade for so many years. We never know how our labors in the vineyard will bear fruit, but we do know we can expect to be pruned and watered.

Reflections:

One of your great virtues is your willingness to grow and improve. You are constantly striving to better yourself. But if your extra efforts go unnoticed, you may become bitter rather than better. To grow, your goal must be to better yourself without regard for what others think. You have to be prepared to be pruned in order to grow more fully. And you have to be willing to share the fruits of your labors.

I'm going to share the fruits of my success with someone today.

DECEMBER 12

"Be not afraid of growing slowly, be afraid only of standing still."
—Chinese proverb

Once planted, a Chinese bamboo seed takes five years to show any visible signs of growth. But beneath the surface of the soil, the germinating seed sends out an elaborate labyrinth of nurturing roots that set the stage for spectacular growth. For the Chinese bamboo grows up to 120 feet within a few months of sprouting.

Reflections:

You never know when a thought that you plant in your heart will sprout and grow. But so long as you keep on watering it, nurturing it with positive imaging and repetition, the idea will take root. Do you want to find balance in your life? New, creative after-hours outlets for your energy? An expanded circle of friends? Plant a seed, nurture it with prayer, and see yourself succeeding. Then watch the idea grow within you.

I have to focus on a long-range goal that is challenging and uplifting, one that will transform my life.

DECEMBER 13

*"Your souls will find rest, for my yoke is
easy and my burden light."*
—Matthew 11:30

In the Bible, the yoke is a symbol of slavery,
bondage, and affliction. But slavery under the He-
brews was as mild as possible in that era. No He-
brew could be a permanent slave of another and had
to be freed, whether or not the debt had been satisfied, after seven years. Many modern executives
slave away their entire careers in a vain attempt to
satisfy some imagined debt or inadequacy.

Reflections:

No doubt you have accomplished a lot and are
capable of doing much more. But at some point you
have to lay down the yoke of power and ambition
and find rest from your burdens. Why not take a few
moments now to visualize yourself succeeding at
some goal *outside* of work. How will you reward
yourself when you accomplish it? A vacation? A
dinner out? Picture the reward in vivid terms, and
it will motivate you to achieve it.

*I have to channel some of my ambition into areas
outside of work.*

DECEMBER 14

"A man without a purpose is like a ship without a rudder."
—Thomas Carlyle

Today's desk-top computers can map out sales territories in color displays that let you realign boundaries with one keystroke. We've come a long way from the Age of Discovery when maps were bordered by elaborate illustrations of dragons, fearsome symbols of uncharted territories. Those who ventured into this *terra incognito* did not fall off the face of the earth, as expected, but discovered vast new territories. There is still a terra incognito waiting to be explored, one that lies beyond the reaches of our computer technology, but within the reach of our spirituality.

Reflections:

Each of us is on a voyage of self-discovery during which there may be many mid-course corrections as we adjust to the shifting current of events. There may be times when you drift off course and lose sight of your goal. But so long as you continue in the general direction that you've charted, you'll reach your destination.

I'm going/to stay the course and achieve my goal of simplicity in all that I do.

DECEMBER 15

"Our God forever and ever; He will guide us."

—Psalm 48:15

During the Bronze Age, sailors feared the east wind because it could blow their low-slung coastal vessels into the turbulent waters of the Mediterranean. Not so the sailors of Tarshish, a city located on the Guadalquivir River in southwestern Spain. Their high-sided, sail-driven vessels did not rely on oar power, but on trade winds and on a single oarsman steering from the stern. The ships of Tarshish were the largest seagoing vessels known to the Semitic world. The city's name was synonymous with sea power; its sailors were in their element in the deep water.

Reflections:

Too often in life we lack the strength to venture out far from the shoreline of our faith. We stay in the shallows, afraid to take risks, make commitments, and work for the long term. As a result, we are buffeted by the pounding surf, rip tides, and hidden shoals of doubt. Only when we accept a Higher Power at the helm do we feel safe in deeper waters.

Deepen my faith; steer me in the right direction.

DECEMBER 16

"With God, all things are possible."
—Mark 10:25

Using a deep-diving bathyscaphe, marine biologists have discovered a subterranean world of fantastic creatures that thrive in the utter darkness and incredible pressure two miles below the surface of the sea. There, jets of superheated water, escaping from fissures, spew lethal chemicals into the Stygian domain. Instead of photosynthesis, these creatures use chemosynthesis to convert the highly toxic water into the staff of life.

Reflections:

To witness these phantasmagorical, whimsical shapes parade forth from the darkness in all their bioluminescent wonder, is to participate in a madcap, otherworldly Mardi Gras. A celebration of life, it is also a reminder of how great and wonderful is our Higher Power. It is not limited by our understanding of its laws. We have only just begun to plumb the depths of its powers.

I have to go deeper in my spiritual life.

DECEMBER 17

"Hell is an endless, hopeless conversation with oneself."

—Dante Alighieri

Sometimes prayer can become a monologue in which we do all the talking, and our Higher Power is supposed to do all the listening. Wordiness in prayer can be a form of distraction in that it makes us self-conscious. We begin to search for the right words, instead of searching for a Higher Power. When Paul said, "Pray without ceasing," he had something much simpler in mind: prayers of the heart.

Reflections:

Prayers of the heart are short, simple prayers, unceasing, all-inclusive, and selfless. they typically consist of a single word of one or two soft-sounding syllables, such as "Amen!" ("So be it"), repeated over and over again in measured breaths for up to fifteen minutes each morning. By repeating the word, or mantra, you take it into your heart. Then you can repeat it throughout the day, especially when you find yourself in a stressful situation.

I have to learn to pray as simply as a child.

DECEMBER 18

*"If we could hear one another's prayers,
it would relieve God of a great burden."*
—Romans 5:3–4

One of the paradoxes of workaholic behavior is the sharp contrast between our boldness in business and our passive, theoretical approach to spirituality. Until now, we've been reluctant to commit ourselves to anything, or anyone, that did not promise an immediate, measurable payoff. But now that we've had a spiritual awakening, we can deepen the experience by sharing our gift with others.

Reflections:

Is there someone at work who is exhibiting the depression, irritability, and lethargy that are symptoms of burnout? He or she may need your help in learning to cope with job stress. The best way to help someone in this position is by sharing your own story and listening to his or hers. In helping that person, you help yourself, and the payoff is fast in coming!

Today, I will go out of my way to help someone at work who seems burnt out.

DECEMBER 19

"The strength of a man's virtue should not be measured by his special exertions, but by his habitual acts."
—Blaise Pascal

As president and chairman of the Board of Minnesota Mutual Life, Harold Cummings led the nation's tenth largest mutual life insurance company. Yet Harold was never too busy to help civic and cultural organizations. Long after retirement, he maintained an office from which he operated as a fund-raiser for nonprofit groups. One clue to his philosophy could be seen on the credenza behind his desk. There stood a pair of bronze boots on a wood plaque that was engraved with the words: "If you want to leave footprints on the sands of time, wear work boots."

Reflections:

There are workaholics and there are workaholics. The first kind are so preoccupied with work they don't give anything back to society. The second kind, people like Harold Cummings, share their success, and, in the process, are richly blessed. According to a Gallup poll, the average top achiever devotes 3.1 hours a week to volunteer work. Those with incomes of $200,000 or more volunteer 4.7 hours a week. One secret of success is the willingness to share it with others.

Today I'm going to volunteer to help one nonprofit group.

DECEMBER 20

"God grant me the serenity to accept the things I cannot change; the courage to change the things I can; and the wisdom to know the difference."
—Reinhold Niebuhr

In the garden of Gethsemane, Christ prayed three time to know his father's will, and each time, when he heard what obedience required of him, he was dismayed. Maybe he wanted more time to bolster Peter's confidence, to relieve Thomas's doubts, and to overcome Judas's cynicism. At one point, he even prayed that "this cup" might be taken from him, then quickly added, "Yet not my will, but thine be done." Christ was an obedient servant.

Reflections:

Sometimes, when we're called to obedience, we may not like what we hear. Have you ever found yourself in a personal review questioning your boss's view of your work? Maybe you thought you had done a good job and expected a big promotion— only to hear that more was expected of you. Maybe you asked for more time to work with a struggling assistant, only to hear that the decision was out of your hands. Maybe you asked for a raise and heard it wasn't in the budget. At times it's hard to accept someone else's point of view. Just ask Christ—he understands exactly how it feels, and he'll listen to you.

Give me the grace to accept a Higher Power's will for my life.

*"Life's greatest pleasure and satisfaction
is found in giving, and the greatest gift of
all gifts is that of one's self."*
—J. C. Penney

The great regret of the terminally ill is not what
they have done with their lives, but rather what they
might have done and didn't do. They are troubled
by missed opportunities and taunted by the words
"If only. . . . " Of all the regrets we might feel, the
most poignant must surely be that we were so consumed by success that we failed to achieve anything
worthwhile and enduring.

Reflections:

When we start keeping score with paychecks
and press clippings, we confuse competing with
achieving. To compete, we must be indifferent to the
needs of others; but in order to achieve something
truly meaningful, we must focus on the needs of
others. Is there someone you've been meaning to
help, if only you weren't so busy? Is there a charity
that could use your time and talents as well as your
money? Why not make a new beginning today? As
Henry Newman once said, "Fear not that your life
shall come to an end, but rather that it shall never
have a beginning."

The greatest need is to be needed.

*"There are two kinds of egotists: Those
who admit it, and the rest of us."*
—Laurence J. Peter

We workaholics can be so preoccupied with our
jobs and business problems that we do not show any
real interest in our co-workers. We often act like the
entrepreneur who, after telling a new hire at length
about his company, said, "But enough about me and
my business. What about you?—What do you think
about my firm?" Yet numerous studies have shown
that company morale and productivity increase
when the boss treats each employee as an individual.

Reflections:

Our spiritual progress begins when we shift our
focus from ourselves to others. It could be a kind
word to someone we meet in the hallway. It might
be a hand-written greeting card on a birthday or an-
niversary with the firm. It could be a short memo
congratulating someone on a job well done. It could
simply be listening to someone else's troubles and
giving them an encouraging word, the Good News.
One sure way to take your mind off your problems
is to commit a Bible verse to heart each morning.
Then repeat it over and over during the day.

*"Be intent on things above rather than on things of
earth"* (Colossians 3:2).

DECEMBER 23

"Prayer is not asking. It is a longing of the soul."

—Mohandas Gandhi

Prayer is work, so much so that most people can't do it for more than fifteen minutes at a time. If you wait until the spirit moves you, you're not apt to pray very often. Pick a set time and place every day. Then put yourself in the right frame of mind with a devotional book. Select a passage to focus on and to interpret in light of the day's events. Let the passage speak to you as though you were listening to the voice of your Higher Power.

Reflections:

One reason why prayer may seem difficult is that we tend to do all the talking; it becomes a monologue instead of a dialogue. In our impatience, we rush to fill the silence with the sound of our own voice rather than let the words of Scripture resonate within us until they strike a responsive chord.

I'm going to memorize one inspirational thought a day so it reverberates throughout my day.

*"Nothing is more simple than greatness.
Indeed, to be great is to be simple."*
                    —Ralph Waldo Emerson

Malcolm Muggeridge reports that over the crucifix in Mother Teresa's convents a sign reads, "I thirst." With those words in mind, the sari-clad Missionaries of Charity devote themselves to a ministry notable for its simplicity rather than its heroics. The staple of their simple diet is five chapattis a day. The only difference between them and those they serve is that the street people were born to poverty, while the nuns chose it freely. "Begin in a small way," Mother Teresa urges them. "Don't look for numbers. Every small act of love for the unwanted and poor is important to Jesus."

Reflections:

Workaholics prefer the heroic, grandiose gesture. Our attitude toward serving others was captured in a cartoon that showed an executive on bended knee, praying: "Oh, Lord, use me, but use me in an executive capacity." We can wait all our lives for the clarion call to service, the herald announcing the nature of our ministry, when all around us co-workers whisper, "I thirst." Does someone at work thirst for an encouraging word from you?

The tongue is the strongest muscle in the human body; with a single word, it can lift someone's spirits for an entire day.

DECEMBER 25

"One friend in a lifetime is much; two are many; three are hardly possible."
—Henry Adams

In extreme cases of workaholism, the person has no close, intimate friends, but merely acquaintances known only superficially and with whom all talk centers around work. True friendship requires sharing on a deeper, more intimate basis, one that entails a genuine feeling of concern. True friendships take time to develop, and workaholics seldom have time for anyone.

Reflections:

How long has it been since you made a few friends outside of work? What efforts are you making to form new friendships? Do you belong to any civic or fraternal organizations? Are you active in your church? Do you participate in your children's activities and neighborhood events? Making friends isn't easy, but if you don't make the effort, it's only a question of time before the few friends you have move on with their lives. In fact, one out of three families move every year, which means that in three years you may have to develop a completely new circle of friends. Are you working at it?

The fastest way to widen our circle of friends is to become active members of our place of worship.

"I have lived to thank God that all my prayers have not been answered."
—Jean Ingelow

It's not uncommon, when you write in your journal, to become distracted by disjointed snatches of thoughts that, unbidden, flit across your conscious mind. If the same thought crosses your mind again and again, you may want to take a closer look at it. There may be an underlying issue there that your Higher Power wants you to reflect on.

Reflections:

Write in your journal the thoughts that are bothering you. By externalizing your concerns and fears, you are better able to deal with them. Having thought about them for a few minutes, close the cover of your journal to block out the distracting thoughts and offer them up to your Higher Power. Then ask for guidance in solving your problems.

Grant me the wisdom to distinguish between real and imaginary problems.

DECEMBER 27

*"Extremists think 'communication'
means agreeing with them."*
                        —Leo Rosten

Sooner or later in writing a journal, we all reach a point where we run out of things to say. The cause of these mental blocks is usually an unresolved problem, or a repressed emotion that we're not ready to confront. It inhibits the free association of ideas that lead to new, spiritual insights. When that occurs, we may be tempted to put our journal aside just when our Higher Power is about to speak to us. For when we become silent, God is ready to speak to us.

Reflections:
One way to open a new channel of communication with your Higher Power is to switch from writing in the "first person" (as though you were talking to a Higher Power) to the "second person (as though it were speaking to you). If it were talking to you now, what would it have to say? Is there an unresolved problem or emotion that you'd like to hear its view on? Ask your Higher Power to speak.

Speak, Higher Power, your servant is listening.

> *"The fewer the words, the better the prayer."*
>
> —Martin Luther

When you started journaling, chances are your ideas flowed freely, covering many pages, and you were pleased at the richness of your own thoughts and feelings, which had until now remained quiescent and unexpressed. But as you continued on your voyage of personal discovery, your entries probably became shorter, more focused, and less self-conscious. Eventually your entries may even have become dry and barren, and you experienced a dark night of the soul.

Reflections:

The key to sustaining your journaling is the spiritual nourishment you get by reading devotional books. Try to set aside time each evening to study the lives and teachings of the mystics. Books such as *The Journal of a Soul* and *The Cloud of Unknowing* can trigger many days of journal entries. But don't confuse the length of your journal entries with the depth of your prayer. Sometimes the best journal entries are those in which we simply say yes to what God is saying to us.

In prayer, it's not what I have to say, but what God has to say, that matters.

*"Hell is full of noise and is probably full
of clocks that emphasize the time that
never passes."*

—Fulton J. Sheen

The clamor and clangor of the business world
is so great that rush hour noise in major cities is at
90 decibels, or 5 decibels above the comfort zone.
The din in many factories exceeds 100 decibels, and
over 16 million people work in conditions unsafe
for their hearing. In numerous offices, the machine
gun bursts of high-speed printers, the jangling of
phones, and the rumbling of copier machines is so
enervating we try to mask it with something euphe-
mistically called "white noise."

Reflections:

Workaholics are drawn to the *sturm und drang*
of business. We revel in the noise, the shouting, giving commands that others obey. To us, silence is
threatening. But we all need a certain amount of silence in which to hear ourselves think and sort out
our ideas. Christ, for example, sought the silence of
the desert before every major passage in his life.
How long has it been since you spent a day in silence and solitude?

*I need silence and solitude to get in touch with my
spirit.*

DECEMBER 30

*"I believe the first test of a truly great
man is humility."*

—John Ruskin

During the Middle Ages, goldsmiths tested for
gold by inserting the questionable ore inside a po-
rous clay cup, which they placed in white-hot coals.
Under the tremendous heat, each element in the ore
liquified at its own melting point, to be absorbed by
the walls of the cup. At last only gold remained,
because it has a higher melting point than the other
ores. When the cup was removed from the fire, its
walls had been strengthened by the absorbed metals,
and inside it contained pure gold.

Reflections:

One sign of humility is recognizing that we are
not strong enough to handle life's problems on our
own. We need help when we're tested in the fire.
Like the wall of the goldsmith's cup, we have to be
open to God's strengthening grace, or we may crack
under the heat and pressure of the changes occurring in business today. In order to refine our talents
and bring out the best in ourselves, we have to be
willing to change as our Higher Power sees fit.

*My goal for today is to accept whatever tests come
my way.*

> *"Riches are not an end in life, but an instrument of life."*
> —Henry Ward Beecher

John Templeton is one of the most successful financiers in the history of Wall Street. His firm manages $9 billion in mutual funds for over 600,000 investors. Yet this self-made billionaire feels his most important investment has been the Templeton Progress on Religion Prize. The world's largest monetary award, the $435,000 prize is intended to call attention to people who have found new ways to increase humanity's love of God or understanding of God. John Templeton believes that true success is based on firm spiritual principles.

Reflections:

John Templeton attributes his success to twenty eight spiritual disciplines outlined in his book, *The Templeton Plan.* While other financiers put their faith in computer printouts, he puts his faith in truthfulness, perseverance, thrift, enthusiasm, humility, and altruism. Judging by his record, they must be good business principles, too.

The only real success is spiritual success.

BIBLIOGRAPHY

Bennis, Warren, and Burt Nanus. *Leaders: The Strategies for Taking Charge.* New York: Harper & Row, 1985.

Benson, Herbert, with William Proctor. *Beyond the Relaxation Response.* New York: Times Books, 1984

Boorstin, Daniel J. *The Discoverers.* New York: Vintage Books, 1983.

Borgmann, Dmitri A. *Beyond Language: Adventures in Word and Thought.* New York: Scribner's, 1967.

Brod, Craig, *Technostress.* Reading, MA: Addison-Wesley, 1984.

Burns, David D. *Feeling Good.* New York: Morrow, 1980.

Flesch, Rudolph. *The Art of Clear Thinking.* New York: Barnes & Noble, 1951.

Freudenberger, Herbert J., and Geraldine Richelson. *Burn-out.* New York: Bantam Books, 1980.

Friedman, Meyer, and Ray Rosenman. *Type A Behavior and Your Heart.* New York: Fawcett Books, 1974.

Gardner, Martin. *Aha! Gotcha.* San Francisco: Freeman, 1982.

Garfield, Charles. *Peak Performers: The New Heroes of American Business.* New York: Morrow, 1986.

Geneen, Harold, with Alvin Moscow. *Managing.* Garden City, NY: 1984.

Hayes, John R. *The Complete Problem Solver.* New York: Scribner's, 1981.

Heller, Robert. *The Super Managers*. New York: McGraw-Hill, 1984.

Hilton, Conrad. *Be My Guest*. Englewood Cliffs, NJ: Prentice-Hall, 1957.

Jenks, James M., and John M. Kelly. *Don't Do—Delegate!* New York: Ballantine Books, 1985.

Kahneman, Daniel, Paul Slovic, and Amos Tversky. *Judgment Under Uncertainty: Heuristics and Biases*. Cambridge, England: Cambridge University Press, 1982.

LaBier, Douglas. *Modern Madness: The Emotional Fallout of Success*. Reading, MA: Addison-Wesley, 1986.

LeBouef, Michael. *Working Smart*. New York: Warner Books, 1979.

Mahoney, David, with Richard Conarroe. *Confessions of a Street Smart Manager*. New York: Simon & Schuster, 1988.

Montgomery, Robert Leo. *Listening Made Easy*. New York: A division of American Management Association, 1981.

Neustadt, Richard E, and Ernest R. May. *Thinking in Time*. New York: Free Press (MacMillan), 1986.

Robbins, Anthony. *Unlimited Power*. New York: Simon and Schuster, 1986.

Rucker, Rudy. *Mind Tools*. Boston: Houghton Mifflin, 1987.

Sculley, John. *Odyssey*. New York: Harper & Row, 1987.

Sheen, Fulton J. *On Being Human*. Garden City, NY: Doubleday and Company, 1982.

Van Kleet, James K. *The 22 Biggest Mistakes Managers Make and How to Correct Them*. West Nyack, New York, Parker Publishing, 1973.

Wriston, Walter. *Risk and Other Four Letter Words*. New York: Harper & Row, 1986.

SUGGESTED READING

Anderson, Andy. *Fasting Changed My Life*. Nashville, TN: Broadman Press, 1978.

Augustine, Norman. *Augustine's Laws*. New York: Penguin Books, 1986.

Campbell, Jeremy. *Grammatical Man*. New York: Touchstone Books, 1982.

Foster, Richard. *Freedom of Simplicity*. New York: Harper & Row, 1981.

Foster, Richard. *Celebration of Discipline*. New York: Harper & Row, 1978.

Frankl, Viktor E. *Man's Search for Meaning*. New York: Washington Square Press, 1984.

Fromm, Erich. *To Have or To Be*. New York: Bantam Books, 1976.

Gwain, Shakti. *Creative Visualization*. New York: Bantam Books, 1978.

Hall, Edward T. *The Dance of Life*. Garden City, NY: Anchor Press/Doubleday, 1984.

Hall, Edward T. *Beyond Culture*. Garden City, NY: Anchor Press/Doubleday, 1981.

Hofstadter, Douglas R. *Metamagical Themas*. New York: Bantam Books, 1985.

Hunt, Morton. *The Universe Within*. New York: Simon and Schuster, 1982.

Maltz, Maxwell. *Psychocybernetics*. North Hollywood, CA: Wilshire Books, 1960.

Murchie, Guy. *Music of the Spheres*. New York: Dover Books, 1967.

Murchie, Guy. *The Seven Mysteries of Life*. Boston: Houghton Mifflin, 1978.

Pagel, Heinz, *The Cosmic Code*. New York: Simon & Schuster, 1982.

Peale, Norman Vincent. *Positive Imaging*. New York: Fawcett Crest, 1982.

Peck, M. Scott, M.D. *The Road Less Traveled*. New York: Simon & Schuster/Touchstone Books, 1978.

Pieper, Joseph. *Leisure: The Basis of Culture*. New York: Random House, 1963.

Prigogine, Ilya, and Isabell Stengers. *Order Out of Chaos*. New York: Bantam Books, 1984.

Rifkin, Jeremy, with Ted Howard. *Entropy*. New York: Bantam Books, 1980.

Ritchie, David. *The Binary Brain*. Boston: Little, Brown, 1984.

Sagan, Carl. *Broca's Brain*. New York: Ballantine Books, 1979.

Thomas, Lewis. *The Lives of a Cell*. New York: Bantam Books, 1974.

Viscott, David. *Taking Care of Business*. New York: Simon & Schuster/ Pocket Books, 1985.

Weiland, James D. *How to Think Straight*. Totowa, NJ: Rouman & Allanhell, Helix Books, 1963.

Woolfolk, Robert L., and Frank C. Richardson. *Stress, Sanity and Survival*. New York: Signet Books, 1978.